Bukowski: OnFilm

NY Times Best-seller
MARC SHAPIRO

For more information contact:
Riverdale Avenue Books
5676 Riverdale Avenue
Riverdale, NY 10471

www.riverdaleavebooks.com

Design by www.formatting4U.com
Cover by Scott Carpenter

Digital ISBN: 9781626016583
Paperback ISBN: 9781626016590
Hardcover ISBN: 9781626016613

First Edition: August 2023

This Book Is Dedicated To My Wife
Nancy Shapiro
(1949-2021)

I am still in mourning. Still sad. Still with the memories. There's so much about you that I miss. Your beauty inside and out. Your kindness. Your loving nature. Your ability to cut to the chase in every way and every day. I miss the big moments. The small moments. The good times. When you wanted to be alone and you meant it. When you wanted to be held and you meant it. I knew your laugh. I knew your cry. When we argued. When we made up. When we were in different places. But still felt together. Now we are apart. But we remain together. In dreams. In memories. The memories of you. Love You Forever. Marc

What they are saying about Marc Shapiro's Celebrity Biographies

All Things Must Pass: The Life of George Harrison

"A well-written and informative volume" - *Record Collector*

"A compelling portrait of the modest musician who... was responsible for the Beatles' transformation from a 60s boy band into a musical force"- *Goodtimes*

"A compelling insight into this great man"- *Bolton Evening News*

Hector Lavoe: Passion and Pain

"Marc Shapiro's Passion and Pain is a matter-of-fact recount of Lavoe's musical glory and tragic life devoid of sensational revelation to make it more sellable." —*NY Daily News*

"A no-holds barred biography..." —*Uptown Magazine*

Annette Funicello: America's Sweetheart

5 stars
"I loved the trip down memory lane. Pulled out her letters, cards, pictures she sent me."
> Jeanette Borderieux, childhood friend of Annette Funicello
> after reading *Annette Funicello: America's Sweetheart*

Justin Bieber: The Fever

"Marc Shapiro ... gives you an unprecedented sneak peak into [Justin Bieber's] childhood, friendships with fellow teen sensations and stories from the road. This new bio is exactly what the loyal JB fan is looking for!" —*CosmoGirl*

"...a very interesting read and a great success story that is very inspiring." —*The Fringe Magazine*

TABLE OF CONTENTS

Author's Notes
I Wrote This

What makes you qualified to write about somebody? Well, it goes something like this:

An abiding interest in the subject, often bordering on obsession. A drive to enlighten and entertain the reader. A publisher who is interested in having me do it. And, of course, there's that old bugaboo about having to come up with the scratch to pay the bills. True confession: I'm that way on all counts. Guilty as charged.

But when it came to writing a book about the author Charles Bukowski, a well known drunk, womanizer, misogynist and all-around not too nice a person, and, almost after the fact, one of the most driven, brilliant and raw creative minds in the history of literature, well you can add one more element to my qualifications. And it's an important one.

First and foremost, I am a fan, and the adulation goes back decades.

I've read almost all of his books (the missing early chapbooks and appearances in lit mags being the most glaring holes in my collection)—most, more than once. The stack of reading material in my bathroom currently features *The Rooming House Madrigals*, *The Pleasures of the Damned* and that classic of dark and dourness: *Erections, Ejaculations, Exhibitions and General Tales of Ordinary Madness*. I was fortunate enough to be in the audience of a rare Bukowski reading at a club called The Golden Bear in Huntington Beach, California, and lived to tell about it. And finally, I was truly honored to have one of my short stories appear along side a Bukowski story in an anthology called *Sleeping With Snakes*. So yeah, I felt truly qualified to write a 'different' kind of Bukowski book—with the emphasis on different.

Some very good biographies by some very talented authors have been written about Charles Bukowski. To a large extent they got it as right as right can be, and have painted quite the accurate picture of the man and his demons. But I did say "different." So here goes.

i

Bukowski: On Film

Charles Bukowski was never a big fan of the movies, and he would be the first to tell you as much, as he recalled in his collection *The Last Night of the Earth Poems*:

"I mostly go to the movies to eat popcorn in the dark."

"People see so many movies that when they finally see one not so bad as the others, they think it's great. An Academy Award means that you don't stink quite as much as your cousin."

But while Bukowski did not care much for the movies, filmmakers from all over the world have loved Bukowski's work which, to date, has resulted in more than 50 film adaptations of his stories, from feature length to short form, from the more well known films like *Barfly* and *Tales of Ordinary Madness* to more obscure films like *Cold Moon* and *Crazy Love*, and finally to the films that have been almost impossible to pinpoint on the map and that are rarely seen.

His often grudging influence and impact on the film world has spanned decades, from foreign filmmakers (for whom the Bukowski books have long been held in God-like stature) to legions of filmmakers on the fringes and student filmmakers on the verge of some semblance of creative coming-of-age and career, whose first tastes of cinematic notoriety were adaptations of Bukowski's works. Even a Midwest 17 year-old, with no money and next to none of the filmmaking necessities, managed to cobble together a primitive, yet darkly evocative interpretation of the Bukowski story "A .45 To Pay The Rent." And lest we forget, there's a goldmine of documentaries on Bukowski, abundant with Bukowski readings and drunken interviews that are legendary in the world of Bukowski completists.

Bukowski, either with his stories as source material, actually writing a script, or, in a handful of cases, appearing in the films, has been "there, done that and bitched about it" to the bitter end. Bukowski, during his

1

lifetime and long after his death, has remained a signpost on the road, and a constant challenge for progressive and, yes, brave filmmakers.

And so you have *Bukowski: On Film,* an up close and personal look at his filmography through his own eyes, as well as those who knew him well, and those who attempted to make cinematic sense of it all. How the films were conceived, complete with wild and zany backstories: how Bukowski was approached by the filmmakers, and his reaction and the background of each film's making.

I like to think of this book as equal parts film survey and historical perspective, light on the uber critical, ivory tower observations, and heavy on Bukowski's evolution in film. And how, for better or worse, he was ultimately treated by those who aspired to capture the essence of the man on film.

This treasure hunt into the land of Bukowski-inspired and adapted cinema was anything but easy. The big studio and higher-level independents were relatively easy to pinpoint, and familiar in concept, if not backstory, to the devoted Bukowskiphile. But the further down the Bukowski slide I went the more difficult research became.

There were a lot of fragments of student films and no-budget independents lurking in the cinematic weeds, a surprising number being early films of foreign filmmakers that went straight from the camera lens to amazing levels of obscurity. It took countless hours of research with a capital R to get what amounted to a passing acknowledgement of their existence. Those often proved a head-scratching nightmare for this Bukowski film completest, intent on finding every last nugget, but wading through the numerous and often obscure films was also very much a Bukowski fans' busman's holiday. I got to get an up close and personal look at how filmmakers dissected Bukowski and his work and made it, cinematically speaking, tick.

To focus on the man and his cinema universe was a daunting task. Some films remained so obscure that everything I found barely filled a page. Others presented details and stories that were surprising and complex: a story within the story, if you will. Many of these Bukowski oddities are readily available on various internet platforms and formats, while others are the movie equivalent of the Loch Ness Monster or Bigfoot. But it was worth the effort, and before you are the results that will most certainly send you on a hunt of your own for those missing links in the Bukowski film universe.

What I discovered in researching this book was that Bukowski, despite his many personality quirks, had a lot of friends, associates and observers who were more than willing to share their anecdotes, memories and critical and personal observations of the man and his work as it pertained to his forays into the film world.

That people were so forthcoming was a happy surprise. When an initial inquiry in Los Angeles turned into an unexpected contact from a poet in Texas who led me to a highly regarded scholar in Spain who had access to literally thousands of pages of Bukowski correspondence, what can I say? Getting people to talk is rarely this easy or rewarding.

At the end of the day, *Bukowski: On Film* is the literary equivalent of a 12-round fight between two aging heavyweights: one in which Bukowski emerges bloodied and battered, but ultimately triumphant.

Free at Last

Charles Bukowski and John Martin met in 1965. Each of them had brought a big piece of themselves to share with the other.

Martin was following his dream to begin his own publishing empire in a mid-life career change. During those dreams of what would become Black Sparrow Press, Martin always sensed that his first author would be Bukowski, somebody who he followed for the better part of a decade. Martin marveled at Bukowski's primitive and powerful work in obscure lit mags and tiny, limited edition chapbook collections. The raw honesty of his words on the page had inspired Martin to take this big step.

"I started Black Sparrow Press to publish Charles Bukowski," Martin said in a *Vice Magazine* interview. "I'd seen his work in underground magazines and I just became convinced, almost obsessively, that he was the new Walt Whitman."

By the time Bukowski and Martin got together, what Bukowski was and would become had been chiseled deep into mental and emotional stone. It seemed to him this meeting was the last stop on his nearly five decade-long journey through the nine circles of hell. From birth, life had been a never-ending horror show, seemingly devoid of any sense of humanity and hope. That molded him into the anti-social outlier who encountered Martin.

Bukowski's sufferings are universally well-known to his followers. His young life was a literal horror show played out in the darkest corners of pre-World War II America, replete with two overriding constants: physical abuse and disfigurement. The abuse he suffered from the ages of six to 11 from his father who would enact a weekly ritual of beating the young Bukowski three times a week with a razor strop, for the most minor and, often, nonexistent infractions. The disfigurement would manifest itself in a disturbing case of acne called Acne Vulgaris, literal boils that over the years would cover his face and body and leave scars.

In a cinematic sense it was the Elephant Man, Frankenstein and Freddy Krueger all rolled into one. In real life it was Charles Bukowski.

Throughout his life, Bukowski would readily acknowledge those two elements of his upbringing as driving forces in his evolution as a writer. He would be of two minds on these matters, often citing the pain he felt as the origin of his life choices. Just as often, as when he offered drunken insights into his life with many beers and a *Rolling Stone* reporter, he would say, "I got pretty hard from all the beatings from my father. The old man toughed me up and got me ready for the world." But, he would add, the pain went deep into his personal psyche. "It was the hatred for my father coming out through the boils in my skin. It was an emotional thing."

There were also the less obvious things that drove Bukowski ever inward. He was shy, socially withdrawn and bullied and shunned at every turn. These were the things that drove him to isolate himself within his many trips to the Los Angeles Library, where he discovered favorite authors and the idea, albeit vague at that point, of becoming a writer.

It was during his early teen years that Bukowski began to drink. Alcohol would ultimately prove to be integral to Bukowski's oeuvre, making him more social and outgoing. Alcohol, he once offered, "helped me to deal with life for a very long time."

After graduating from Los Angeles High School and attending Los Angeles City College for two years, Bukowski dropped out and moved to the East Coast where the legend of Henry Chinaski, his alter ego, would be born in a number of poems and short stories written in fleabag rooms and in his off hours from soul crushing menial jobs, and the beginning of his sexual adventures with questionable women. For Bukowski, this period of self-discovery was the essence of this character: a born outsider living a dissolute life. And Bukowski would cultivate that image throughout his own life, too.

Bukowski would see his first story published at age 24 when *Story Magazine* published "Aftermath of A Lengthy Rejection Slip." Two years later a second story, "20 Tanks from Kesseldown" found its way into issue three of *Portfolio: An Intercontinental Quarterly*. But the lack of consistent success soon began to weigh on Bukowski, and it was not long before he gave up writing in favor of what he recalled as "a ten year drunk" in which he roamed the US, living in countless flea bag rooms, taking on an endless array of dead end jobs and, occasionally, running afoul of the law. A legendary run-in with the United States government over accusations of draft evasion—a case built largely on the fact that he had a German accent—resulted in Bukowski spending 17 days in jail before a psychological examination proved that he was unfit to serve.

Bukowski came off the road and back to Los Angeles in the early 50's, falling into a hardscrabble sense of stability. He got a job with the Post Office as a fill-in letter carrier, a position he would hold for three years and, depending on what stories one believed, he either stopped drinking all together or cut back considerably. But by 1955, Bukowski's life had evolved into chaos and drama.

He married a small town Texas poet named Barbara Frye. Not surprisingly, the marriage was made in hell. Bukowski and Frye were of equal temperament and tolerance in all the wrong ways. The tumultuous marriage lasted three years and ended in divorce. About the time the marriage was falling apart, he checked himself into the hospital to deal with a bleeding ulcer, most likely brought on by his hard life style and drinking.

Bukowski spent days in the hospital fighting a bleeding ulcer condition that those treating him felt might well kill him. But Bukowski pulled through, and rather than seeing the light, he immediately went back to the dark side. He began drinking again, but during this latest downward spiral he was brought back to what had been his on-again off-again passion: writing, and, in particular, poetry. It was a poetry that reflected Bukowski's rage, frustration and the futility of his life to that point. He was turning out jagged bits of verse—often little more than thinly disguised rants, and sending them out to magazines. Rather than the mountain of rejections he had come to be used to, his evolving style was suddenly beginning to find acceptance along the small-circulation lit magazine superhighway, with such magazines as *Gallows, Nomad* and others running his poems with regularity.

Bukowski returned to the Post Office in 1960 with the less physically demanding, but no less mind-numbing position of letter filing clerk. His anti-social attitude toward the job, his fellow workers, and the hopelessness of his life would manifest itself in endless drinking and womanizing. Perhaps most importantly, in his burgeoning literary life he was dealing with his growing acceptance of his "life is shit and then you die" approach to writing.

Hearse Press would publish Bukowski's first separately printed

7

story, a broadside entitled "His Way The Painter" in June 1960, and would follow with Bukowski's first chapbook *Flower, Fist and Bestial Wail* in October of the same year.

Bukowski's already notorious reputation with women was unexpectedly sidetracked in 1962 when he met and fell in love with a woman ten years his senior, Jayne Cooney Baker. Bukowski was still Bukowski, but Baker had softened him for the first time in his life. When Baker died unexpectedly in 1964 from a burst stomach ulcer Bukowski was devastated, and would go on to devote a whole series of stories and poems to his feelings about her passing.

In an excerpt from one of Bukowski's poems dealing with Baker's death, entitled "To Jane Cooney," which appeared in the 2002 collection *Open All Night*, the poet was at his most reflective and melancholy.

and so you have gone
leaving me here
in a room with a torn shade
and Seigfried's Idyll playing on a small red radio.
and you left so quickly
as suddenly as you had arrived

Bukowski's more domestic side would surface in 1964 when a baby girl named Marina Bukowski was born to the writer and his live-in girlfriend at the time, Francis Smith. The relationship with Smith did not last, but Bukowski would prove to be, as much as was humanly possible by his own standards, a doting father, being in his daughter's life and being consistent in paying child support.

By this time Bukowski, in terms of style, had rounded into shape. His poetry was hard edged, free verse that focused on sex, violence and the absurdities of life. His short stories were raw, observational and thinly veiled exercises in observational biography, often told through the life experiences and misadventures of Henry Chinaski. And it was a style that continued to find favor with the small, independent presses. A regular convert to the Bukowski oeuvre was Loujon Press, who ran Bukowski in their literary magazine *Outsider* and would publish early chapbooks *It Catches My Heart in Its Hands* in 1963 and *Crucifix in a Deathhand* in 1965.

Bukowski continued to be emotionally and spiritually crushed by the mind-numbing job at the post office. It cultivated his extremely anti-social nature on the job that often saw him having run-ins with superiors.

His life away from the job served only to cement his attitude as an often mean-spirited loner whose existence seemingly revolved around squalid living conditions, drinking, regular trips to the racetrack and womanizing.

Bukowski turned 49 in 1965, and was at the crossroads. There had been a modicum of success through publication in little magazines and small presses but the reality was it was the post office that was paying his rent. But emotionally and otherwise, it was the post office that was grinding his life to dust. Finally, he made a pivotal decision. In a letter to German editor Carl Weissner which appeared in the collection *Living on Luck*, Bukowski stated, "I have one of two choices. I can stay in the post office and go crazy or stay out here and play at writer and starve. I have decided to starve."

Fortunately Bukowski's decision would coincide with the decision of John Martin to, likewise, follow his passion as he slowly began the process of weaning himself away from his job as a manager of a Southern California office supply company in the hopes of starting his own book publishing enterprise. Martin made it his mission to track down Bukowski and to lay the groundwork for publishing his work. Not surprisingly, Bukowski was skeptical but Martin, after a series of meetings over a six month period, convinced the writer that he was legitimate.

Martin recalled the moment when Bukowski and he sealed the deal with *Vice Magazine*. "We sat down with a little piece of paper. I sat there with a pen and he listed out all of his monthly expenses. This was 1965. His rent was $35 a month. He had $15 for child support, $3 for cigarettes, $10 for liquor and $15 for food. He could get along on $100 a month. I was only earning $400 a month at my regular job, so the agreement was that I was giving him 25 percent of my income."

The deal called for Bukowski to be paid that $100 a month for life whether he wrote anything or not. Given Bukowski's well-earned reputation, Martin knew he was taking a chance. But what he counted on was Bukowski's desire and dedication and a rarely seen decency and honesty. Martin had given him the excuse to finally quit the post office and do nothing but write and he was sincere in his desire not to double cross him.

Right after inking the deal with Black Sparrow, Bukowski gave his notice at the post office. He was nothing if not business like in sealing the deal with Black Sparrow. He worked at the post office until December

31 and then told Martin that he was going to take January 1, 1966 off for a holiday. But he was quick to indicate "That I am going to start working for you on January 2."

Shortly after signing with Black Sparrow, Martin released the company's first Bukowski, a limited edition of 30 copies of the poem "True Story" in April 1966. With Black Sparrow now doing the grunt work of printing and growing a distribution network that was willing to take Black Sparrow books, Bukowski was free to write.

In addition, Bukowski would also find an outlet for his pent up life in 1967 when he began penning the weekly column "Notes of a Dirty Old Man" for the Los Angeles underground paper *Open City*. It was Bukowski at his primitive best: a mixture of his true-life misadventures and daily comings and goings that showcased the author as an amazing storyteller and writer capable of inspiring both pathos and laughs. So "Henry Chinaski" stumbled through his days and nights. As an outgrowth of "Henry Chinaski," Bukowski created the name "Hank," which he came to use to define his own alter ego.

When *Open City* folded, "Notes of a Dirty Old Man" was picked up by *The Los Angeles Free Press*, ran for another two years and showcased Bukowski's notorious life and creative talents to a rapidly expanding audience.

Martin and Bukowski would converse constantly, and during one such conversation in January 1970 Martin suggested that Bukowski might consider writing a novel, as poems and short stories are usually a harder sell. Bukowski took the suggestion literally. Three weeks later, Martin received a phone call from Bukowski who said, "Come and pick it up." Martin said "What?" to which Bukowski replied, "My novel. You said write a novel." Martin was amazed. "How could you write a novel in three weeks?" Bukowski said, "Fear."

The novel was *Post Office*, a semi autobiographical look at Henry Chinaski's years in the Los Angeles Post Office. It was rough, raw and profane. But above all, *Post Office* was real life as filtered through the life and ingrained futility of the author. *Post Office* was a powerful first step in the direction of mass acceptance.

And it would not be long before the filmmaking community started noticing Bukowski and started coming around.

Cherkovski on The Mythic Monster

Neeli Cherkovski knows more about Bukowski than most. As an up and coming poet on the scene in the 60's, they would regularly hang out, share many beers together and just talk about the hard, honest life of a poet whose words and life pulled no punches. In fact, Cherkovski is, despite a long, distinguished career as a published poet in his own right, so tied to his relationship to the legendary "Dirty Old Man" that he is quick to utter "Oh! Bukowski, again!" when approached by this author to yet again offer up bits of Bukowski lore. But the naturally good-natured and accommodating poet quickly warmed to the idea of once again pontificating about his good friend and sharing his memories of their olden days.

Bukowski was hard to get to know, and getting into his inner circle and staying there was a constant challenge. Cherkovski, who would go on to write the biography *Hank: The Life of Charles Bukowski*, and would co-edit, with Bukowski, the short lived and noted literary magazine *Laugh Literary and Man The Humping Guns*, recalled what brought him and Bukowski together.

"I was an up and coming poet and a heavy beer drinker in the 60's who did not want anything from him." He said that even being a close friend of Bukowski was a challenge. "He could be a very difficult friend. Not an impossible friend. Not an outrageous friend. But a very difficult friend. He could be very paranoid and almost wanted to be disappointed in people."

Cherkovski chuckled as he recalled one bit of irony when, during one of many beer-soaked conversations, Bukowski told him quite seriously, "I've become a mythic monster who can do no right or wrong."

That comment was an understatement when it came to Hollywood and the film industry's seemingly unrelenting attraction to Bukowski. An attitude that Cherkovski is quick to point out is that it was not reciprocal.

"Generally he [Bukowski] despised most movies. *All Quiet on the Western Front* was his favorite movie. It dealt with glory in a way he liked. But for the most part, he couldn't understand why people liked them. He was such a narrative writer, and he didn't like the narrative in films. He thought they [film narratives] were simple and idiotic. Across the board, he didn't trust the film industry. It was too much of a business and it was too involved in the business. It wasn't, to his way of thinking, involved in creativity and art. It was about the bottom line, and he didn't like that."

Cherkovski agreed with the popular notion that at the root of Bukowski's dislike for the movies was the fact that because of his scarred face, he had an emotional ax to grind with the so-called "handsome, pretty boy" actors that populated the films. "I imagine his physical appearance had something to do with that. Because of his scarred face, I would imagine that was true. He didn't like the pretty boys at all." Cherkovski described Bukowski addressing the issue on one occasion when he told him, "Before I became well known, I had a scarred face from a bad acne operation. Then when I became known it was 'the face of genius.'"

Cherkovski knew Bukowski when the film people started coming around. He cited Taylor Hackford's Bukowski documentary as ground zero for the movie industry's interest and he was privy to those early sales of film rights to his earliest books. Many critics have been quick to paint those early film deals by Bukowski as a "cash grab." But Cherkovski explained that, while light years from wealthy, Bukowski really did not need the money. "He really did not need the money and he was not a greedy guy. It was just that little extra money coming in, and that's why he got involved in film."

Cherkovski stifled a laugh at the suggestion that Bukowski secretly harbored acting ambitions, and that was the main reason he went after film offers. "I can tell you for sure that he did not want to be an actor. His act was his act. He was sick after he would do those poetry readings and, afterward, he would tell me 'I made a clown of myself. I got up on stage, I made a clown of myself and I got $1,500.'"

But he did concede that there was a magnetic quality about Bukowski's character, and that his written work was like catnip to a legion of, largely, European filmmakers. "It's the stories that he wrote, and his personality. Alcohol and sex: that's what Hollywood saw in him, and he wasn't like that. He once told me 'Hollywood thinks I'm a sex genius. Man, I've got them fooled. And now the young ladies come and they force themselves on me. It isn't me. It's an idea of me.' Hollywood saw that, and they yearned to be rough and tough artists. I think some of the filmmakers wanted to be Bukowski. But I think most of them wanted to make use of Bukowski. They wanted to get into his skin and make money on it."

Cherkovski also offered that Bukowski's vision of America was very much in vogue with Europeans, and aligned with their impression of the US. "People in Europe liked Bukowski because his poetry was like dirty dishwater in a pan. He would get up in the morning and say, 'Motherfucker!' and that's the way Europeans like to think of America."

At the end of the day, Cherkovski is adamant that the dance between Bukowski and film was simply mercenary. "I think he would be rather disdainful of the films made about him and his work. I think a lot of it had to do with the commerciality of it all. Just like there's a lot of books out on Bukowski: Bukowski on drugs, Bukowski on sex, Bukowski on drinking. Bukowski had become a commodity to Hollywood, and not a poet. All of that was stupid to him. And Bukowski ran away from everything stupid."

Bukowski at Bellevue (1970)

At a time when most people are somewhere beyond middle age and reflecting on whatever the future might bring, Bukowski, in 1970, had turned 50, and was suddenly faced with a celebrity of sorts, and a burgeoning career as a poet. His books were receiving critical and international acclaim, and his royalties had quickly outpaced the monthly "allowance" that John Martin at Black Sparrow was giving him.

The one thing that Bukowski dreaded with a passion was reading live. He did it out of necessity to earn an extra buck. His reputation, and the rabid nature of his followers, had already cast the Bukowski experience in stone: inevitably it would be raucous, confrontational and bordering on literary anarchy. Bukowski pulled no punches in his travelogue of a reading experience in a piece entitled, "Would You Suggest Writing as a Career?" in the collection *Erections, Ejaculations and General Tales of Ordinary Madness*. In an airport bar he let fly on the subject of reading live.

"The readings I don't like. They're stupid. Like digging a ditch. Like digging a ditch. It's survival. I'd hate to get lynched for reading a sonnet."

Bukowski knew from experience. A few days earlier, he was the ringmaster in two readings at a local Los Angeles bookstore that had gone according to form: a winged literary combat that hovered around the edges of chaos. But here he was, on his way to the Pacific Northwest for yet another round of insanity, heading for a reading at Bellevue Community College. Literary professor and huge Bukowski fan Carl Waluconis had fronted Bukowski's airfare and helped to provide a hefty, by the writer's standards, reading fee. This would be the first time Bukowski had ever flown in an airplane—which was just another excuse to get roaring drunk before the flight. He would have loved to skip out on the gig, but he had already cashed the check. And Bukowski was, if nothing else, a man of his word. The flight and its concomitant days and nights of drinking and partying would not be surprising to anybody familiar with his at large reputation as a hellraiser. This was captured in manic detail in his story, "Would You Suggest Writing as a Career?" "We didn't crash," he said of his very first airplane ride. "I had my second allowable drink. Then I sneaked an extra one. A full glass. Straight down. No water. Then we were there. Seattle."

Bukowski had initially been scheduled for a reading at Bellevue Community College, but agreed to a preliminary reading at Washington Community College. Bukowski was uncomfortable, and, most likely, well into his cups when he took the makeshift stage before an equally uncomfortable and unaccustomed-to-his-brand-of-real-life audience. An after party followed: a drunken blow out in which Bukowski recalled making out, apparently with the tacit okay of all parties, with the wife of the professor who had arranged the reading.

The next day, it was a drunk and uptight Bukowski who made his way to the Bellevue Community College reading. Things went even further down hill when Bukowski was informed that a local TV show would be filming his performance.

Bukowski recalled in "Would You Suggest Writing as a Career?" that he might be in for a rough ride when, shortly after sitting down in a chair on the stage, he was approached by the TV show cameraman who advised him that when he held up his hand, Bukowski should begin. Bukowski would recall that he was in a panic at that moment. "'I'm going to vomit,' I thought. I tried to find some poetry books. The guy held up his hand. I began. My name is Chinaski. First poem is called…"

Four poems into the one hour performance, Bukowski hit a thermos he had brought on stage with him. It wasn't coffee, but it did have the desired effect of making his reading a bit more tolerable for himself and an audience, who seemed more into it than the previous days.

Bukowski at Bellevue, which would lay largely unseen before surfacing in 1995 on Netflix, on video and, in the coming years, on countless websites, would prove to be a relic of some note. Bukowski was uncomfortable and stiff in his performance; what passed for between-poem patter was garbled. Bukowski was far from being a polished performer, and it showed. But the grainy and largely unfocused VHS recording would succeed in capturing the power of Bukowski in the early days: raw, to the point, powerful examples of just who Charles Bukowski was and what, creatively, he was all about.

The significance of *Bukowski at Bellevue* has often been debated. Yes, the camera work was Stone Age, and the performance was, depending on who one talked to, either very bad or brilliant.

Dennis Schwartz at *DennisSchwartzReviews.com* commented that, "Despite the poor visual quality, the soundtrack on this one hour reading comes through loud and clear. This is a defining moment in the poet's career." Critic Phil Hall of *Film Threat.com* simply acknowledged *Bukowski at Bellevue* as "A treat for Bukowski addicts." But it would remain for critic Terry Trueman at *Medium.com* to cut to the chase with his assessment. "It's obvious that he doesn't want to be reading in a room full of confused and nervous college kids. He's discovering that he doesn't enjoy this part of fame at all."

Bukowski seemed to sum up the significance of *Bukowski at Bellevue* shortly after finishing the reading, as chronicled in "Would You Suggest Writing as a Career?" "I seemed to have gotten away with it. Who cared? Just get me out alive."

Bukowski (1973)

Filmmaker Taylor Hackford knew Bukowski well. He had found the writer in the pages of the underground newspaper *Open City*, and had cultivated a friendship. They would go to the racetrack together and would spend many a days in downtown dive bars getting drunk. For Hackford that friendship evolved into something more. He would come to look upon Bukowski as a mentor.

"I always thought Bukowski was an absolute iconoclast who did things his way," he said. "He didn't give a shit. He turned his back on success."

Hackford and Bukowski's friendship would flourish in the early 70's. For Hackford it was a time of finding himself as a creative—in the mailroom of the Los Angeles-based public television station *KCET*. "When I was working in the mailroom, somebody asked me one day if I could shoot film. I lied and said I could, and ended up not screwing things up too badly."

Hackford remained in Bukowski's world, and was witness to the publication of *Post Office* in 1971. Seeing the cinematic potential in the book, Hackford negotiated a deal with Bukowski for both the film rights to the book and the rights to the name Henry Chinaski. It was a stealth deal whose particulars remain unclear to this day. But it would lay the groundwork for Bukowski's first celluloid adventure.

Hackford recalled that KCET was expanding its long-form journalism and, in particular, pieces on people, particularly artists who had ties to Southern California. Hackford approached the company with the idea of doing a cinéma vérité look at the life of Charles Bukowski. Most had not heard of Charles Bukowski but trusted Hackford's instincts and insights, and green lit the project.

Bukowski greeted the news with the expected amusement and cynicism. Being basically shy in public, he was not sure about how it would be having a camera crew follow him around, but he trusted Hackford and agreed to the idea. Hackford's approach to filming Bukowski would be minimalist in the extreme. His budget was miniscule, and with that in mind he decided to shoot the film in black and white. Hackford knew that a black and white format would reflect his subject's personality.

What Hackford had in mind for the documentary was following Bukowski through his day on the dark side of town, roaming his neighborhood and getting up close and personal in his home. Those scenes would be sprinkled with Bukowski relating stories of his time in the post office and his approach to his style of writing poetry. The film would also document Bukowski at the racetrack, discussing his approach to betting. There was also the added tension to contend with of Bukowski's current girlfriend, Linda King, and Bukowski cheating on her as the filming played out.

As directed by Richard Davies, Bukowski came across as quite natural, telling his stories in a matter of fact manner. As he would later acknowledge, he was well aware of the camera crew stalking his every move, but it did not seem to intimidate him.

"Taylor Hackford showed up with a camera man [Richard Davies] and I guess he was the director," recalled Bukowski in *Malibu Magazine*. "They decided before they shot the film that we'd get drunk together four or five times to get to know each other and to take the pressure off. They just kind of followed me around. The camera was there all the time. I'd go into a liquor store and there they'd be. I'd go to the races and they'd be there too. I'd been going to the track for 20 or 30 years and now, all of a sudden, there's a camera following me around with equipment, a girl holding a mic and a guy with a camera."

Shortly after beginning filming *Bukowski* (the working title at that point), an unexpected curve ball was thrown into play. Lawrence Ferlinghetti, considered one of the founding fathers of the beat movement and who ran the famed flash point for the era's most influential writers— City Lights Books in San Francisco, offered Bukowski the opportunity to fly to San Francisco to give an hour-long reading, an invite that came with an honorarium of $400 and all expenses paid, including airfare and hotel room. Hackford thought that seeing Bukowski live in front of an adoring audience could be the crescendo of the documentary.

Bukowski was less than enthused. He had stage fright when it came to readings, rarely doing them, and when he did he preferred the audience never top 20 people. He would drink to excess just before a reading, and would vomit just before a reading would begin. Now faced with what Ferlinghetti predicted would be an audience of 800, the $400 would be the dealmaker, so he agreed.

The camera was rolling as an already drunk Bukowski boarded the plane to San Francisco. Bukowski acted the drunken fool on the short hop from Los Angeles to San Francisco, spitting profanities and vile rants throughout the flight, unnerving other passengers. Hackford, who had designated himself as the documentary interviewer, attempted to ask some questions during the flight, but it soon became evident that what would be best for the film would just to film "Buk" being Buk.

Backstage at the City Lights reading, Bukowski was in truly rare form, not only throwing up before the reading started, but vomiting on stage in front of a rabid audience who cheered and jeered every misstep. Bukowski would alternately read, yell at the audience and take pauses to swig beer. More spectacle than literary event, the reading was a distillation of everything the poet had become known for: the angst, the anger, the self-destructive and deathly outlook on life. It was all there for Hackford and his film crew to record for posterity. Bukowski left the stage to thunderous applause and drunken cheers and jeers. The audience was just as drunk as Bukowski was and, as Bukowski performances go, it was one for the ages.

After the reading, Bukowski held court in a hotel room for local luminaries and people who had, more or less, been invited to join the poet for late night hijinks. The camera continued to roll late into the night. The alcohol-fueled party turned ugly. A fight broke out between two of the partygoers, and the result was that a window was broken. Bukowski was by this time way past the legal limit and exploded in a profanity-laced argument with his girlfriend Linda, who finally had enough and left. With the release of the documentary, the San Francisco trip succeeded in holding Bukowski up to the world to see this budding legend in all of his surreal glory.

The filmmaking experience between Bukowski and Hackford appeared cordial and cooperative. Bukowski never said no to filming the numerous indelicate moments, and projected a "bring it on" attitude that resulted in the raw footage being gold. But things unexpectedly went south shortly after they returned to Los Angeles.

21

Bukowski wrote a piece for the *Los Angeles Free Press* about the San Francisco trip in which he excoriated Hackford and the filmmakers as "punk stupid asshole filmmakers," and that he had done all the organizing and logistics, and that the filmmakers "would bumble along, asking stupid questions." Hackford read the article and exploded. He immediately tracked down Bukowski and confronted him. What follows of that exchange is an excerpt from the website *Bukowski Quotes.com*.

"I told him, 'Hank… I read that article.'"

Bukowski responded, "Yeah baby, what'd you think?"

"I said I thought it was full of shit man," said the angry Hackford. "You forget I have the film. You're the guy who's drunk on the plane, making a fool out of yourself, and you made me out to be an idiot."

Bukowski in a biting retort said, "Hey baby, when I write I'm the hero of my shit. You got your film, you do your film."

Hackford did just that, and on November 23, 1973, *Bukowski*, a one hour documentary, aired on *KCET*. Not unexpectedly, people chose sides on the film's relative merit. The sheer rawness and profane real-world vision made a lot of viewers cringe; the documentary literally pummeled the senses. And it was those same elements that had just as many people hailing it as a masterpiece.

But it would remain for no less an organization than the Federal Communications Commission to truly validate Bukowski's maiden voyage into cinema. The element of profanity had been so pervasive that complaints were filed from many quarters with the FCC. After due deliberation, the FCC dismissed the complaints…

Because in their eyes, Bukowski was art.

Close But No Bukowski (1972, 1977-1982)

Bukowski was shaping up as a literary icon by the time Taylor Hackford filmed the afore described writer's notorious meltdown in 1972. His books were beginning to sell at a fairly brisk clip. His outsized persona was capturing its first rush of headlines and controversies. Bukowski was on the verge of becoming "somebody" in the public consciousness. And, as it often happens, people started appearing out of the proverbial woodwork, hoping to land a seat on the Bukowski train before it left the station.

Bukowski's relationship with the film world was quickly turning into the Bukowski wild wild West. Veteran author Howard Sounes, who penned the biography *Charles Bukowski: Locked in the Arms of a Crazy Life*, had a sense of what was going on. "As well as being full of would-be novelists, the world is also [filled] with would-be filmmakers," he stated, describing the environment at the time. Bukowski was selling rights to his published works on a whim, and those who were not willing to cough up money for legitimate rights would regularly buttonhole Bukowski with ideas of their own. Stories of such film projects that would ultimately be DOA, but, in the telling, they often proved interesting.

Doing research for his own book, Sounes discovered one of those would-be Bukowski aspirants was rock musician Marty Balin, member of the legendary group the Jefferson Airplane. Sounes heard the skinny from Balin himself, and told the story accordingly. "Marty Balin told me he had written a film script which was inspired by Bukowski, whose work he greatly admired in the 1960's/early '70's. Not sure, but maybe he adapted something specific Bukowski had already written, maybe something from *Notes of a Dirty Old Man*—which would be the right period."

Sounes went on to describe how, as told to him by Balin, the musician crossed paths with Bukowski on the night of Bukowski's documented meltdown. "Marty Balin said that he took his script to show to Bukowski at Lawrence Ferlinghetti's apartment after the reading in San Francisco.

Marty certainly met Bukowski at the aftershow, piss up with the intention of trying to work with him on a movie. But Bukowski was not in a receptive state. He was drunk, and having a fight with his girlfriend. Marty said that he was more interested in Marty's girlfriend than literary talk. I think Marty was disappointed and a little annoyed that Bukowski did not take him seriously. And the project never really went any further."

But as Sounes would discover, this would not be the end of that story. Some years after the night in question, and shortly after the author interviewed Balin, Sounes was in for a surprise. "After he told me his story [in 1996], Marty Balin's dad/manager unexpectedly airmailed me a copy of the script—from San Francisco to London. I'm sure I read it at the time out of politeness, but, to be perfectly honest, I can't recall any details now. Perhaps the Balins thought that perhaps I could help them get it made all those years later. All I can say is that hope never dies."

On a slightly higher level, there was an early '70's to early '80's attempt by Taylor Hackford, who had bought the rights to Bukowski's first novel *Post Office* long before Bukowski was considered somebody, as early as 1976 was in active talks with Playboy Productions to make the film, which, according to never-substantiated reports, may have had Sean Penn in the title role of Henry Chinaski. There were reportedly three different drafts of the script during the lifetime of the negotiations, according to records at *The Bancroft Library (University of California)* dated 1976, 1977 and 1982, written by the late writer Don Carpenter, along with semi-serious back and forths between Playboy and Hackford, and Hackford and Bukowski, on how it should be handled.

According to the book *Visceral Bukowski: The Sniper Landscape of L.A. Writers*, Hackford was inclined to go along with the idea of *Post Office* as an anti-war cinema polemic. Bukowski said no.

What is known is that the back and forth with Playboy Productions would apparently run its course between 1977 and 1982 before Playboy would finally say "Thanks, but no thanks," and walk away from *Post Office*.

And finally, the seemingly endless saga of Hollywood attempting to make *Women* into a movie continued to go nowhere in fits and starts. In 2015, *Tracking Board.com* trumpeted the latest attempt, when it announced that Voltage Pictures now had the film rights to *Women* and that there was actually a script written by one Ethan Furman. Almost as an afterthought, no director or cast had been named at that point.

Seven years later, *Women* had not been made.

Supervan (1973)

Bukowski was Bukowski in 1973. He was drunk, unpredictable, angry, anti-social and an emerging womanizer of some notoriety and legend. It was any combination of the above that also made him impulsive and willing to try anything for a laugh or kicks. Or to get drunk and get laid. 1973 would be the year he met filmmaker Lamar Card and, in typical Bukowski manner, would make his acting debut.

Filmmaker Card was notable for his low budget, cheesy exploitation films that never strayed far from the tried and true formula of sex, violence and a lot of teen car action hijinks. Enter Supervan: a teenage romp involving fast cars, a souped-up van, bikers, babes and the inevitable corrupt politicos and corporate types—the stereotypes that push all the right buttons in hormone-driven youth. This was typical grade B stuff.

And in B we mean Bukowski. Uncredited and with no dialogue, in one scene he plays a drunken letch who, as "Wet T-Shirt Contest Boy," sprays questionably-legal teen girls with a hose and buckets of water, and at one point fondles one of the girls. Bukowski, on screen for a reported 1:10 of running time, had very little to do. Acting as a dirty old man was a role he could definitely handle.

Typical of these kinds of films, Supervan was in and out of theaters so fast that it barely had time to get its expected critical brickbats before it disappeared into the void of what was film archives in the early '70's. Consequently, how Bukowski wandered into this movie remains largely a mystery. Even those who considered themselves Bukowski experts were shocked to find out about this film.

There is an urban legend on that account that has been circulating for some time. Reportedly, Bukowski, who happened to be in Missouri where the movie was being filmed, had been pursuing a young actress who had landed a part in Supervan, and when he arrived on the set the filmmakers thought it would be cool if this dirty old man, for all intents and purposes, played himself.

Truth be told, the invitation was not quite so dramatic. As reported in a *Sussex University* thesis by J.C. Farhoumand, it was as simple as the director Lamar Card inviting Bukowski to play up his image as a dirty old man and Bukowski agreeing. The film finds Bukowski doing a raunchy bit of fondling of the breasts of the girl, who in real life may well have been the girl of his dreams. An overdubbed musical soundtrack accompanies the action, and, for the record, Bukowski does not have one word of dialogue. But he grins a lot.

Supervan, ultimately, is throwaway stuff, but with Bukowski was slowly but surely forming into the shape of a pop culture "next big thing," this breakthrough film role was priceless.

The Great Film Director (1975)

Most assume that Bukowski's only written shot across the broadside of film was his late-in-life book *Hollywood*. But he would occasionally take often veiled, but in a large sense, obvious shots in his poetry. "The Movie Actors," which appeared in *Jacaranda Review*, was an early work that took dead aim at his perceived idea of the frailties and insecurities of those in front of the camera. But easily the most biting attacks on film came in 1975, while writing his *Notes of a Dirty Old Man* column for *The Los Angeles Free Press* when, with the poem "The Great Film Director," he let fly, without naming names.

> This guy was so out
> I went to see him
> When I was in New York
> He was on the tenth floor
> And there were 40 people in the apartment
> Talking and vomiting
> And fingering each other
> Drinking out of huge jugs of cheap wine
> And passing pills
> One guy threw a flower pot out a window
> Another pissed a long yellow stream of urine against a mirror
> The director was in the center of the rug
> Surrounded by toothless 17 year old girls
> I asked for his autograph
> Got it
> And left

Charles Bukowski: East Hollywood (1976)

Bukowski's willingness to accommodate creative types would run hot and cold. Sometimes he just wanted to be left alone. But occasionally, depending on how he was approached and his feeling about the person he was dealing with, he could be surprisingly open to letting people probe his most private moments. Such was the case when he received a letter from European documentary filmmaker Thomas Schmitt.

This was a time when Bukowski was in transition. Professionally, his life was growing by leaps and bounds. His books were selling quite well in the United States and internationally. Personally, it was a whole other story. His tempestuous relationship with Linda King had come to an end, and he was now very much involved with Pamela 'Cupcakes' Wood. His notorious East Hollywood digs were growing tiresome, and Bukowski, in keeping with his growing status, was contemplating moving elsewhere.

Schmitt would capture some truly rare and intimate looks at the life of the poet in the documentary's 55-minute running time, cavorting in and around his home and East Hollywood haunts with Pamela, and offering up what many insist was the first on camera reading of the notable Bukowski poem "The Shower."

Like most Bukowski films of that period, *Charles Bukowski: East Hollywood* would be shown sporadically at first, finding a sizeable audience in Germany. But also, like Bukowski's early films, word of mouth and the critical approval of this black and white wonder would prove to be a time capsule of sorts of the period in Bukowski's life where he was coming of age as a poet, and anything was possible.

Hello I'm Back: Bukowski in Hamburg (1978)

Bukowski had been big in Europe long before he caught on in the United States. And it was no surprise that he had those occasional moments of longing to discover his birthplace in Andernach, Germany. The stars would align when Bukowski was offered a reading in Hamburg and, as it would turn out, to have de facto Bukowski filmmaker Thomas Schmitt tag along to for the second stage of his cinematic Bukowski trilogy, creating *Hello I'm Back: Bukowski in Hamburg*.

Bukowski was, typically, at wits end in his personal life, having recently broken up with Pamela 'Cupcakes' Ward and taken up with a seemingly more compatible (that is, prone to heavy drinking and excessive behavior) Linda Lee. But Bukowski made his way through Europe, with a pit stop for a chaotic French interview, en route to the Hamburg reading and the stopover in Andernach, and Schmitt found the turmoil in Bukowski's life largely replaced by a sense of contentment. Bukowski and Lee on a boat ride down a river in Germany and the nostalgic meeting with long lost family members in Andernach, captured rare moments of Bukowski at peace.

The Hamburg reading was well received. To be sure, the film is peppered with enough of the usual Bukowski antics, the drunken lashings out and such. But by film's end with see Bukowski in a state of ragged grace. *Hello I'm Back: Bukowski in Hamburg* was seen on German television before making its way to international fans. It falls into the semi-obscure category and has often commandeered a price well into the hundreds. But for many it might just be worth the price of admission to see moments of Bukowski close to being normal.

There's Gonna Be a Goddamned Riot in Here! (1979)

By 1979, Bukowski, by his standards, was living high on the hog. After years of struggle, he was finally making enough money off royalties from book sales and a couple of movie rights deals to allow him to stop doing live poetry readings. But that did not mean he could not be tempted.

Dennis Del Torre had been writing Bukowski. He was a big Bukowski fan who offered the poet an all expenses paid trip to Vancouver, British Columbia to read at The Viking Inn before what he assured Bukowski would be a sold out and fanatic audience. Bukowski, sensing that this might be the way to bow out of the live reading life with all guns blazing, agreed under the condition that he get a copy of any recordings made of the reading.

Bukowski was in good spirits as he flew up to Vancouver for the October 12 show. And not surprisingly, his pre-show ritual of getting blind drunk before hitting the stage was already in order, as he would relate in the book *Living on Luck: Selected Letters 1960's-1970's, Volume 2*. "Read to 680 at Viking Inn. Standing room only. Drank before the reading and four bottles of red wine during."

As it turned out, the local college video crew hired by Del Torre would chronicle two hours of what many Bukowski historians would consider Bukowski's finest hour as a live poet. Bukowski was drunk and in attack mode as he read a searing series of new and old poems to a crowd that was, likewise, out for blood. Between poem patter was a literal torrent of vindictiveness as Bukowski and the audience exchanged profanities, threats and a sense of electric tension. This was a Bukowski reading that reflected his life and the scars that were on display. And it had been captured for posterity.

"Not bad," Bukowski reflected in the book *Living on Luck Volume 2*. "Much fighting with the audience. New poems. Dirty stuff. Read the poems out." And he was emphatic at the end of the reading when he told the audience, "I'll never do another of these readings again." *There's Gonna Be a Goddamned Riot in Here!* was to be the filmed result.

But shortly after the reading the tape would be reported "either lost or stolen" by producer Del Torre, and the particulars of its disappearance would be the subject of much speculation. "Time and circumstance had shuffled it off to a back corner where it was forgotten," Del Torre lamented in *Bukowski Forum*. The mystery would remain until 2008 when the late documentary filmmaker John Dullaghan, who at the time was researching his own Bukowski documentary *Born into This*, stumbled upon a copy of the tape at the home of Bukowski's widow, Linda.

Dullaghan immediately sensed that he had stumbled onto something significant and, in short order, became a go between Linda Bukowski, Del Torre and Monday Media producer Jon Monday. Dullaghan returned the tape to Del Torre and negotiated a deal with the producer that would allow him to use part of the tape for his documentary *Born into This*. An agreement was subsequently made between Linda and Monday Media to restore the tape, turn it into a respectable DVD and distribute it.

The response to *There's Gonna Be a Goddamned Riot in Here!* was overwhelmingly positive, capturing Bukowski at his savage, uncompromising best. If this was truly Bukowski's last live performance, it would have been a send off that would live for the ages.

As it turned out, it would be a mighty big if.

Why Bukowski Gave Hollywood the Finger

When Bukowski had a bone to pick, be it with society or something deeper and personal, he would usually find himself at his typewriter, exorcising his demons with a short story or a poem. Hollywood in general and the film industry in particular was a whole other matter. That was a boil that would take a 12 gauge needle to lance. Hence the book *Hollywood*, in which Bukowski chronicled his adventures and misadventures in the film business as fiction, which were not very far from his own truth.

"I guess I never really believed Hollywood," he told *The New York Times*. "I had always heard that it was a horrible place. When I went there I found out how really horrible it was. It was black and cutthroat."

Around the time *Barfly* would cement the interest of Hollywood, Bukowski, in a letter that appeared in the collection *Reach For The Sun*, was at his most vitriolic when addressing his perception of filmmakers as self-absorbed bottom feeders when he said, "I've spent too many nights now with movie people who talk about camera angles and producers and directors, who go to baseball games with Jack Nicholson, kissing his ass, trying to get him to act in their movies, when they really should be kissing the ass of his agent."

But, as he would relate in a *Film Comment* conversation, his dislike was gradual. As a child of the depression, Bukowski thought that Buck Rogers and Tarzan "looked pretty good." *All Quiet on the Western Front* would hold a particular place in his psyche, as would the likes of *One Flew Over the Cuckoo's Nest*, *The Elephant Man* and *Eraserhead*. Those films aside, Bukowski's attitude toward cinema was decidedly disapproving.

"No I don't like movies," he offered *Film Comment*. "It's embarrassing to see a movie. I feel gypped sitting there with all those people. I feel mugged by watching a movie. I feel they take something away from me."

Bukowski would let loose with both fists on the subject of films in a passage of his book *All Quiet on the Western Front*, which featured the illustrations of Robert Crumb. "I will listen to or read the critics. "A great movie," they will say. And I will go see said movie and sit there feeling like a fucking fool, having been robbed and tricked. I can guess every scene before it arrives and the obviousness of the characters, what drives them, what they yearn for, what is so important to them is so juvenile and pathetic. So boring, gross, the love bits are galling, old hat, precious drivel."

Bukowski's distaste for the movies would take on many forms. Howard Sounes, author of the Bukowski biography *Locked in the Arms of a Crazy Life*, said it all boiled down to his feelings about reality and fantasy. "For Bukowski, it wasn't the Hollywood of the film business, it was the rough end of East Hollywood where the working people lived that interested him," he told this author in a 2021 interview. "He had no interest in Hollywood until he saw that he could make some easy money at it. Bukowski was interested in the real life of Hollywood, not what people like John Wayne were doing."

It would turn out that Bukowski's antagonistic attitude toward the movies may well have had its roots in no small amount of jealousy, and may also have had psychological roots. Joan Jobe Smith, a writer-poet and editor of the publications *Pearl* and *The Bukowski Review* who had that rarity—a platonic relationship with Bukowski during the '70's and well into the '80's—echoed the opinion. "The Bukowski I knew hated the movies. He never went to them in the 70's when I knew him. And a big reason for that was that he was jealous of the pretty boy movie stars, especially Cary Grant and Warren Beatty."

One moment that seemingly typified Bukowski's war with Hollywood took place in September 1985 at a birthday party for the wife of photographer and Bukowski-confidant Michael Monfort. As described in the biography *Charles Bukowski: Locked in the Arms of a Crazy Life*, it happened like this: Arnold Schwarzenegger was there, and for no particular reason other than he felt like picking a fight, Bukowski went up to Schwarzenegger and called him a piece of shit. In the book, actor and Bukowski friend Harry Dean Stanton underscored the incident when he said, "Hank was certainly not overly impressed with any of it."

The notion that Bukowski was always seemingly at war with the film industry is the stuff of screaming put downs and 60 point headlines, and to hear Abel Debritto tell it, all the controversy may well have been simply a matter of smoke and mirrors rather than reality. Debritto, a Fulbright scholar and editor-at-large for the books *Charles Bukowski on Writing*, *Charles Bukowski on Cats*, *Charles Bukowski on Love*, *Essential Bukowski*, *Storm for the Living and the Dead* and author of the book *Charles Bukowski King of the Underground*, has spent years pouring over thousands of pages of Bukowski correspondence, and attempted to set the record of Bukowski's war with the film industry straight.

"I don't think he was a frustrated filmmaker or actor," reflected Debritto. "He hardly ever discussed movies in his correspondence or interviews. Bukowski didn't say much about the movie industry unless he was involved in some film project. But when he did he largely put movies down. He felt most actors were oversensitive and prima donnas."

Bukowski biographer Sounes may well be the harshest critic of what Hollywood has failed to do in its cinematic attempts at doing right by the author. He made no bones about it. "Bukowski is a very funny writer. Most filmmakers don't get that across. I thought *Barfly* was terrible, and *Tales of Ordinary Madness* was pretentious. *Factotum* was better, but all of those films were more or less failures because Bukowski's books work due to the writing. It is his sharp, witty, economical use of English that entertains the reader. That doesn't translate into the picture on the screen. The plots of his books are slight. It's the writing that shines."

Bukowski would continue to use nearly every opportunity to take pot shots at the film world which, to a certain degree, was feeding him. During a moment from the documentary *Bukowski: Born into This*, excerpted by Quick Park.com, he let loose with both barrels: "I found out that Hollywood is more crooked, dumber, crueler and stupider than all the books I read about it. They didn't go deeply enough into how it lacks art and soul and heart, and how it is really a piece of crap. There are too many hands directing. There are too many fingers in the pot. They're all kind of ignorant about what they're doing. They're greedy and they're vicious. So you don't get much of a movie."

Bukowski Writes a Screenplay (1979)

By 1979, Bukowski was seemingly entering a new phase in his cinematic journey. Everything to that point had been largely a cash grab, a series of documentaries and filmed readings that, while effectively portraying the Bukowski persona, often left much to be desired when it came to exploring Bukowski the writer and the power of the stories he told.

But that was about to change. Bukowski was, by this time, a successful writer of books whose audience saw something beyond the drunk, womanizing caricature the previous films had showcased. They saw heart, soul and insight beneath his raw exterior, and, in quick order, they had become fans and devotees of his work. Among those was European film director Barbet Schroeder, who had long been the darling of the European film community for helming the likes of *Maitresse* and *Koko: Le Gorille Que Parle*. Schroeder was a fairly recent convert to Bukowski's work, and saw endless cinematic possibilities in the author who told tales of the down and out. In 1979 Schroeder decided that he wanted Bukowski to write a screenplay for him to produce, and set about tracking the reclusive and angry writer.

According to a Bukowski letter in the book *Living on Luck*, Bukowski and Schroeder had crossed paths in Paris during his European homecoming, and had gotten together at his home in 1978 and had bonded over good talk and a lot of drink. In a letter dated August 24, 1978, Bukowski described the moment that Schroeder popped the question.

"He wants to do one of my long short stories as a 90 minute work. I don't know if I have anything that might fit that length."

Schroeder would remain persistent in his pursuit of Bukowski, who said, in an interview in *Film Comment*, "Barbet just kind of showed up one day and said he wanted to make a film about my life. He kind of talked me into it." In reality, he did not have to do all that much talking.

"It came at a pressure time. I was living in a dive and just barely getting by. That's why I did it."

Locked in the Arms of a Crazy Life author Howard Sounes reasoned that Bukowski had only two reasons for agreeing to pen *Barfly*. The obvious one was money. "Whenever filmmakers offered him option money he took it. But he got sucked into the process of making *Barfly* because, quite simply, he liked Barbet Schroeder."

Another element of Bukowski's tumble into the screen trade went this way:

Schroeder would be persistent on the matter, and called Bukowski out of the blue one night and asked him to write a screenplay for him. Bukowski might well have not known who he was talking to, but immediately hung up. Schroeder called back moments later, and, before Bukowski could hang up again, said "$20,000 is the amount I am willing to pay you for a Bukowski-penned screenplay.

By January 1979, Bukowski, who did not know a screenplay from a hole in the ground, was hard at work.

"It's just dialogue," Bukowski smugly observed in *Film Comment*. "It's just people walking around talking."

And as Bukowski would acknowledge in looking back on those days in *L'Europeo Magazine*, he had no interest in learning the finer points of the craft. "To study screenwriting seemed repulsive to me. I think it would have taken away some of my natural impulses and instincts. I prefer the rough to the polished."

Bukowski set to work on the screenplay with the working title of *The Rats of Thirst*, a look at Bukowski in his early grim days when there seemed no hope or future. In a April 23, 1979 letter to friend Carl Weissner collected in the book *The Captain is Out to Lunch and the Sailors Have Taken Over the Ship*, summed up the through line of *The Rats of Thirst* as only he could: colorful and over the top. "It's a short section of my life when I sat around on bar stools, starving and crazed. The screenplay is fairly violent but accurate and it might be humorous. Although I never intended it to be any of those things. I don't know what I intended it to be."

Bukowski and Schroeder were in touch throughout Bukowski's maiden voyage as a screenwriter. Going in, Bukowski had played hardball with the director, insisting, in the contract, that nothing in the script could be changed without his permission. Beyond that, theirs would be a healthy and easy give and take, by Bukowski's standards. By March 1979, Bukowski, in a letter collected in the book *Living on Luck: Selected Letters 1960's-1970's Volume 2*, proclaimed, "No problems with Barbet, yet. I've agreed with his criticisms except in a couple of places where he did not quite understand what I was doing."

For his part, Schroeder was finding working with Bukowski a much easier exercise than his previous films, where he literally was on top of all aspects of the process, with a big portion of making the film the agonizing over story and screenplay. "I took a big step with *Barfly*," Schroeder told *The New York Sun*. "I was freed from having to write my own screenplay. Suddenly I was not left alone with screenplay anxieties."

Bukowski proceeded with the writing of *The Rats of Thirst* at a very un-hurried-by-Hollywood pace. In a letter in the *Living on Luck* collection he disclosed that by March 24, he was "rewriting the screenplay, taking out the bad first parts." At the beginning of April, Bukowski acknowledged that, "it was taking longer than expected." On May 1, he reported that *The Rats of Thirst*, now called *Barfly*—for the sake of Hollywood's conservative attitudes, was completed.

At that point Bukowski, reluctantly, fell prey to the bane of any writer's existence: the rewrite. Schroeder, while quite happy with the results, was a stickler for certain things that he felt the script for *Barfly* had to have. Bukowski would bitch about the rewrite process, but his growing loyalty to Schroeder, not to mention the promised backend of the money once the film went into production, ended with Bukowski fixing elements of the script. This he related in a 1986 letter to John Martin from the collection *Reach for the Sun*:

"There are certain rewrite problems with *Barfly*. I have to go over it and fix it up, one total character in particular. But at least I'm working on my own shit."

In the same letter, Bukowski, showing his naivety to the workings of the film world, would grouse at the inconsistency of the medium. "On *Barfly*, there's still to be more tinkering with the script because it's too expensive and too complicated to shoot certain scenes. If I had known this from the beginning, I would have set the whole thing up in a bar à la a stage play. Of course then they would have said show us something outside the bar."

The script went to Schroeder, who was now on a journey through the international film investing community to get funding to make the film. This left Bukowski to savor the fact that he had written his first screenplay, and now all he could do was wait. "I got $10,000 for writing the damned thing, and there's more to come when and if it gets to shooting. There still remains enough madness and confusion to get me through."

Joan Jobe Smith Remembers Bukowski That Way
(1973-1985)

Joan Jobe Smith was that rare woman in the Bukowski universe. She knew him intimately, but not sexually. Not even once.

"I knew him since 1973," Smith, a multi degreed, former go-go dancer turned author, poet, founder of the internationally acclaimed literary magazine *Pearl* and founding editor of *The Bukowski Review*, an all-Bukowski all-the-time website, told this author. "We were platonic friends. We talked on the phone a lot. I was what you call a feminist loyalist. I was attracted to Bukowski in a sweetheart sort of way. My last phone call from him was when he was writing *Barfly* in 1985. Twelve years we were friends."

Smith would be very much in Bukowski's inner circle when all the important and well-publicized women in his life came and went, and stayed. "Bukowski didn't have much confidence as a teenager," she said, looking back on Bukowski's sexual awakening. "He had acne that turned to boils. From what I understand, he was celibate through his 20's. He finally found his confidence as a handsome man in the 60's when he started to get famous. That's when he started to attract women, and that bolstered his ego. In his 30's, he actually started to look pretty good."

And because she was an important, supportive and, yes, non-sexual cog in the Bukowski wheel of his life and times, Smith was privy to Bukowski's earliest dalliances with film.

"He did not go to the movies as a kid. He read books. He liked writers. One of the main reasons he didn't like the movies was because of all the pretty boy movie stars like Cary Grant, and that dislike came from what he perceived as his own physical appearance. But he was attracted to the idea of movies in their written screenplay form."

But Smith joins the chorus of those who acknowledge that Bukowski was, in the 70's, always quick to sell off the film rights for the proverbial quick buck. "He was interested in Hollywood as a way to make money. He was a tightwad at the time. He wanted money. He really wanted money. It was a cash grab for sure. Plus he wanted to see his story and his character (Henry Chinaski) on the big screen. The ego and insanity of Hollywood appealed to him, but the main thing was the money."

At the other end of this movie love affair was the constant attraction of young filmmakers and, in particular, European art house types who were near reverential in their mania for Bukowski and his world. "The younger guys enjoyed his persona," reflected Smith. "He had been without women most of those days. It was his character Henry Chinaski who did a lot more fun stuff than Bukowski ever did in real life. It was a matter of ego and jealousy with a lot of these filmmakers because they wanted to be like him. The notion of Bukowski and his stories was real cool in the 70's. For the filmmakers, his writing was interesting and sensual. When a character in his story went into a bar, you felt like you were going in there with him. When he would describe the act of fellatio in detail, it wasn't so much porn and eroticism as it was romantic and sympathetic. The Italians and the Germans loved Bukowski because they felt that Bukowski's style was very French, very Truffaut and Goddard."

Smith watched throughout the '70's as the mania for all things Bukowski on film mushroomed. While *Tales of Ordinary Madness* and a handful of documentaries failed on a commercial front, they propagated the notion of Bukowski and his world as something special to be honored and applauded. For her part, Smith recalled that Bukowski's long dormant ego suddenly knew no bounds. "He got rich in 1978 and he was pretty full of himself. By the time *Barfly* would come around, he expected that he would make a lot of money."

One thing that survived his sudden celebrity was that Bukowski, when it came to the films being made about his work, would be loyal to the people who had come to him early. "Loyalty was what it was all about," said Smith. "He wanted his people."

Such was the celebrated case with Barbet Schroeder who had approached Bukowski early on with the *Barfly* concept and the opportunity for Bukowski to write the script and have final say on all the creative decisions connected to the film. It was the time when Hollywood and the film celebrities of the day were attempting to curry favor with the always skeptical Bukowski. There was the notorious intrusion of Sean

Penn and Dennis Hopper, the former Bukowski liked and the later he could not stand, who attempted to take over *Barfly* but were rebuffed rather rudely and crudely on several occasions. The most well-known being the near brawl that ensued one night when Bukowski said some unkind things about Penn's wife Madonna. Long story short, Penn angrily leaped to his wife's defense and a fight seemed imminent before Bukowski backed him down with a very street threat.

Around the time that Smith's relationship with Bukowski was cooling down to its final days, she laughingly recalled how Bukowski put the shame on Penn in one last egregious act. "We were at a party and Bukowski came onto Sean Penn's mother. He was drunk and he went over to Penn's mother and started kissing her and feeling her up. Penn saw what was going on and there was very nearly a brawl.

"Things could get very ugly when Bukowski had been drinking."

The Last Straw (1980)

Bukowski hated poetry readings, and less than a year removed from the events that produced *There's Gonna Be a Goddamned Riot in Here*, he was even more entrenched in the thought that he would never again go before a live audience. Soon, however, the mercurial poet would change his mind.

In 1980, general manager at upstart record label Takoma Records Jon Monday was ramrodding the re-issue of a recording of a Bukowski reading in San Francisco that had initially been released in 1974. Takoma had high hopes for the re-release, and wanted a promotional video of a Bukowski reading to help spark interest and sales. The label approached the poet who, surprisingly, agreed to one more live session for the camera, to be called *The Last Straw*.

Monday was hesitant. He knew Bukowski by reputation, and a pre-reading press event saw Bukowski erupting into a drunken scene, including a food fight and abuse being heaped upon the waiters and assorted press notables. In preparing the video shoot, Monday was prepared for the worst possible scenario.

The reading was set to take place at The Sweetwater Club in Redondo Beach, California. Monday was anxious. "I took my semi-pro video camera and set up in the back of the room, and plugged into the sound board for the audio. Then I settled in for a stormy night. Bukowski took the stage and it was obvious that he had a head start on the drinking. Then it began. A full assault on the audience who gave it right back at him."

From the opening poem, Bukowski was a dervish of drunken anger and abuse. He was constantly picking fights with members of the audience, and at one point pulled out a knife and threatened a heckler. Jon Monday captured it all for posterity and infamy.

The Last Straw was shown around to help promote the release of the spoken word album, but then the film disappeared into the dark corners of Monday's collection. One of those privy to that footage was European filmmaker Barbet Schroder who proclaimed, "This was the best live footage of Bukowski ever!" That rave notice aside, *The Last Straw* would remain in limbo until 2008, when Monday pulled it out, and, like the previous *There's Gonna Be a Goddamned Riot in Here*, struck a deal with Linda Bukowski to digitalize and release *The Last Straw* commercially.

An often vile, 74-minute tension-packed exercise in poetry and chaos, *The Last Straw* made the perfect companion piece to *There's Gonna Be a Goddamned Riot in Here* and stands as testament to Bukowski at both his best and worst.

And the time, Bukowski was as good as his word when, at the conclusion of *The Last Straw*, he yelled out over the rabid audience, "This reading is now over." It would be the last time Bukowski ever read live.

Every Man for Himself (1980)

Bukowski's distillation of his movie experiences: the novel *Hollywood*, is fiction in conceit only. The reality is that only the names have been changed, for reasons known only to Bukowski, and even the name changes are so obviously drawn that it is no secret to anyone even remotely familiar with the author and his movie adventures who he is talking about. In this case the character Jon-Luc Modard is real life filmmaker Jean-Luc Godard.

"John Luc kept right on talking," he described in *Hollywood*. "He was being dark and playing genius. Maybe he was a genius. I didn't want to get bitter about it."

According to *Hollywood*, Godard kept right on talking until he got around to the point. "'Listen,' said Jon-Luc. 'What I want to ask you to do is to write the English dialogue for the subtitles of my new movie. Is it a deal?'"

Bukowski knew that Godard had made an effective contribution to his growing list of celebrities and quasi-celebrities who liked to hang out and drink. In film circles, mostly in Europe, at the time Godard was known as an art-house filmmaker, primarily for his low budget, politically charged, wildly introspective and experimental small films. His name then was barely known outside of Europe.

The request he made from Bukowski was for what was, for Godard, an important reentry for him into films for the masses: *Every Man for Himself*, a complex story of love and relationship, heavy on introspective dialogue and taut, meaningful moments. Whether he liked it or not, Godard was looking for a renewed sense of commercial relevancy. People in the seats. Money in the box office. But the approach to *Every Man for Himself* was very much in the European motif, very art house, id-driven by degrees, and with a taut Euro cast that toplined Jacques Dutronc, Isabelle Huppert and Nathalie Baye.

On the surface, it seemed that Bukowski would be the ideal creative foil to add directness and earthy moments. Bukowski, in a letter to fellow poet and longtime friend Gerald Locklin that originally appeared in *Home Planet News*, outlined how the process would work. "I can't speak French. What happened was that a Frenchman translated the script into English and then I took the English script and I Americanized that."

Godard was quite satisfied with Bukowski's adaptation of the script, and in the end would prove more or less faithful to his Americanized version. Bukowski's influence went a long way toward Godard's attempt to make what he felt was a true Hollywood movie. But, at his core, Godard had his own European attitudes that would result in some tweaks to Bukowski's work. Bukowski, in his writing, made liberal use of American idioms and references that Godard, for the most part, would replace with what he felt were references more accommodating to a European audience. A handful of scenes in the final Bukowski script would be either altered or totally replaced. Of particular note was a sequence in the Bukowski version in which the film's protagonist, after a confrontation with a hotel desk clerk, stabs him with a switchblade, cuts off his penis and flushes it down the toilet. In Godard's hands, that self-same scene was transformed into a much more sedate sequence, in which the male lead drives away in a car while the desk clerk screams after him.

Bukowski would have no problems with the changes. But one thing that did rub Bukowski the wrong way was when he discovered that Godard had used a voiceover of a segment of his poem, "The Most Beautiful Woman In Town," over a scene in the completed film. And, as he explained in a letter to poet Gerald Locklin in *Home Planet News*, he was not amused.

"Godard used one of my poems for a movie scene, and I don't get credit for that. Except one night we were drinking together, and he handed me this batch of (French) francs. " Bukowski took the money, but was still not happy. "That's cash. Not credit. Ok."

Tales of Ordinary Madness (1981)

Bukowski and the movie *Tales of Ordinary Madness* was a tale of two screenings, and, in a very literal sense, of two Bukowski's own tales.

As described in Lionel Rolfe's book *Literary L.A.*, Bukowski had made his way to an early, little publicized and not very well attended look at *Tales of Ordinary Madness* in a West Los Angeles movie house With a brown bag of cheap wine in tow, he made his way to an inconspicuous row of seats as the theater lights went down.

Tales of Ordinary Madness's first scene seemed to cut to the heart of Bukowski and his world. Actor Ben Gazzara, playing the drunken, womanizing poet Charles Serking, the thinly disguised version of Henry Chinaski, fills the screen and immediately takes a swig from a wine bottle inside a brown bag. Bukowski immediately sensed the sense of bonding with his cinematic self and took a swig from his own brown bag wine bottle.

Bukowski reportedly had had some reservations about this first full length motion picture centered around his work. He really had no idea how Hollywood worked, and so his unease at dealing with filmmakers and the associated dealmakers was palpable. "I don't really know how the whole thing happened," he told *Cultural Daily.com*. "It happened quite suddenly. We signed a contract and the next thing I knew I was drinking with Marco Ferreri and Ben Gazzara, and we were talking to each other like we had known each other for years. I guess this is the way things happen."

Bukowski's comment glossed over the fact that his first dealings with Hollywood had, initially, not been the best.

He had been of two minds about Gazzara playing Serking. He had brought the necessity of the character name change on himself when, years earlier, he had signed away the rights to the name Henry Chinaski to filmmaker Taylor Hackford. He was also a bit miffed that City Lights

Books, who had published the book *Erections, Ejaculations, Exhibitions and General Tales of Ordinary Madness* had taken it upon themselves to sell the movie rights without his permission and participation, and he hated that. Adding insult to injury was the fact that Bukowski had not yet received his money from the film rights before filming had begun. In a letter to Black Sparrow Press publisher John Martin, Bukowski unloaded his ire at the Italian filmmaker and his producer with the angry comment, "The Italians… Hitler didn't trust them either."

One of the Italians in this case was director Marco Ferreri, whose reputation had been built around a mixture of art house and European introspective dramas, as well as often farcical comedies such as *La Grand Bouffe*, *La Haren* and *Dillinger è Morto*. That Ferreri or other filmmakers and readers would gravitate toward Bukowski's work is not a surprise, according to Bukowski biographer Sounes, who offered up his reasoning why:

"I suspect that Bukowski's undermining of the American Dream, so to speak, appeals to liberal-minded Europeans who see a lot that is wrong with American society. Bukowski's stories are, on one level, very simple, with lots of good dialogue, and are written in an economical style. That is very appealing. Especially when it came to what Ferreri envisioned as the storyline to *Tales of Ordinary Madness*."

In the book *Laughing with the Gods*, Ferreri would acknowledge that the attraction for the filmmaker was not so much the creator, as it was the work. "I fell in love with Bukowski's books rather than with Bukowski. That's the key with my movie. I was interested in the places, the images, and I found in the States the very images he had caused me to imagine. What appealed to me were those images, those characters, those streets and homes where they lived. The Los Angeles he writes about."

The film follows the sexual and drunken exploits of poet Charles Serking as he navigates the sleazy backwater neighborhoods of Los Angeles in a constant downward spiral of hopelessness, loneliness and debauchery. Along the way he meets Cass, a hooker whose self-destructive habits easily match his, making the pair the most unfortunate of couples in a dark and dismal world. Their relationship is stormy and often violent, but, somehow, it works. Their relationship hits a snag when Serking gets a big bucks publishing offer. Cass tries to stop him from leaving, but fails. Serking soon realizes that he has made a mistake and returns to Los Angeles, only to discover that Cass has killed herself. A cathartic drinking bout ends with Serking rediscovering his passion for poetry and life. On paper, *Tales of Ordinary Madness* appeared solid Hollywood: tragedy and redemption, set against the backdrop of a dark and desolate world.

Ferreri would do due diligence in casting the often shadowy and conniving, agenda driven women that populated Bukowski's stories. For *Tales of Ordinary Madness* his casting choices were literally international. Ornella Muti, already an established Italian film actress, had recently broken through to US audiences in the 1980's *Flash Gordon*. Years later, she would appear in the 1989 movie *Wait until Spring, Bandini*, the film adaptation of a book by Bukowski's favorite author John Fante. Tanya Lopert, a solid representative of the French cinema was also a subtle emotional counter. Last, but certainly not least, was the award winning, and often controversial and troubled fringe character actress Susan Tyrrell.

Bukowski sensed that *Tales of Ordinary Madness* was on the right track and, although he would remain leery of Ferreri's creative intent, he was happy with Ben Gazzara, a rugged, old school actor who had crafted a working man persona in early '60's television, in particular the series' *Arrest and Trial* and *Run for Your Life* as well as a number of studio films. Gazzara also carried with him a sense of art house European in his choices, especially in his work with John Cassavetes. Bottom line, Gazzara, where it counted, had the right chops to pull off Bukowski's alter ego, and seemed a good fit to play Serking.

When the production came to Los Angeles to film, a meeting was arranged between Bukowski and Gazzara, a feeling-out process to see where each of them was at in regards to the film, and how to play Serking a la Bukowski.

As chronicled in the book *Locked in the Arms of a Crazy Life*, Bukowski and Linda Lee showed up at Gazzara's hotel room, several bottles of French wine in hand. The two seemed to hit it off, according to Gazzara. "I think that he was proud that we were making a film about him, but low key proud. He had this sardonic sense of humor that precluded his gushing about anything. But I think he was excited by it."

During their conversation, Gazzara did his best to offer a reassuring defense of how he planned on playing Bukowski by not playing Bukowski. "Not having lived with him to study his mannerisms, I had to invent my own. I didn't go for putting the pock marks in the skin and doing the makeup to uglify him. I thought the important thing was the artist, the interior man."

Bukowski would adopt a "wait and see" attitude during the making of *Tales of Ordinary Madness*. He was curious and wanted, to a large extent, to be surprised. Bukowski, at his drunken and most critical, did not hold out much hope of any branch of Hollywood getting him right on film.

As reported in detail in the books *Literary L.A.* and *Locked in the Arms of a Crazy Life*, *Tales of Ordinary Madness* had its official premiere in 1981. Lots of Bukowski fans were in attendance and Bukowski, Linda Lee at his side, did not disappoint, showing up very drunk and disparaging even before the film began. On the surface, the film seemed to hit Bukowski and his world, with lots of drunkenness, womanizing and, in the case of the character Cass, more than a touch of masochism. Bukowski, sitting in the crowded theater and nursing a brown bag bottle of wine, was openly attacking the film at every turn.

He thought the scene in which Serking continues to write while a willing woman lays on his bed offering her favors was totally unrealistic. He openly complained for everybody in the theater to hear that the apartment sets (scenes which had been filmed in Italy) were too clean and sterile to be his real world hovel. The premiere was marked by Bukowski's seemingly continued diatribe, and eventually one of the people in the audience made the mistake of shushing him.

"Hey I'm the guy they made the movie about," he yelled. "I can say anything I want!"

"Shut up!" came out of the darkness.

"You shut up."

Sometime after the screening, Bukowski, who had seemingly been alright with Gazzara's performance, did an about face. "He had appealing eyes like a constipated man sitting on the pot straining to crap."

How good or bad *Tales of Ordinary Madness* was depended on the critics. They loved the film in Europe, not surprisingly gravitating toward the mixture of art and pornography as well as the Don Quixote nature of Bukowski as he tilted at the windmills of life. The US was less kind, dismissing the film as maddeningly uneven, giving the odd aside to Gazzara's seeming ability to channel the essence of Bukowski.

To Bukowski, *Tales of Ordinary Madness* was an inconsistent mess that he roundly dismissed in several interviews over the years, including a denouncement in *L'Europeo Magazine*. "I didn't like the movie made from *Tales of Ordinary Madness*. It was all out of focus. I hardly recognized it as something taken from my works. The whole thing was just dumb. Almost all of it was worse than bad."

Years later, his disappointment with the film would continue, bringing the combative side of the writer out with all guns blazing in conversations with the magazines *Twisted Image* and *Film Threat*. "That film was a piece of wet shit flopping in the wind. It was to puke."

But even he had to concede in a *Film Comment* interview that putting Bukowski on screen was no easy task.

"I never thought that anyone would do my life story," he told a *Film Comment* interviewer. "I did think that, well maybe I'll die sometime and somebody will take a shot at it. But usually they fuck it up."

Poetry in Motion (1982)

The 1982 documentary *Poetry in Motion* was equal parts anthology and quite effective time capsule of a time when poetry had once again become something of importance. 70 poets and 47 hours of footage was filmed in San Francisco, in Toronto, and at *The St. Marks Poetry Project* in New York City—which has long held the well-earned reputation for being the Woodstock of poetry spaces. Such luminaries as Allen Ginsberg, William Burroughs, Robert Creeley, Diane Di Prima, Gary Snyder, Jim Carroll, Ed Sanders and Tom Waits were filmed reading poetry and doing other non-poetic things for the then 23-year old filmmaker Ron Mann.

"Trying to tell people I was making a film about poetry, people thought I had lost my mind," Mann recalled in an interview with *Poetry Foundation*. "I make films to meet my heroes."

Although it was never quite explained to what degree Bukowski was Mann's hero, during the filmmaking process it was determined that having an interview with Bukowski was necessary. "Along the way, I did a four hour interview with Hank over many bottles of wine," he told *Poetry Foundation*. That interview was largely filed away until filming was completed and Mann set about giving some semblance of structure to the film. The interview with Bukowski was brought out, viewed and discussions were held. In a sense it was typical Bukowski, railing away at the norms and conventions of poetry.

"We were looking for something to kind of anchor to what we had, kind of an anti-narrator," Mann offered *Poetry Foundation*. "Bukowski hated poems and he hated readings. He was exactly what the film needed."

Mann's intuition would prove spot on. While the legendary poets strutting their creative stuff for Mann's lens was quite enticing, and an invigorating document of the poetic times, Bukowski's commentary, sprinkled throughout the film, was a jolt, an in-your-face counter to the film's prevailing and, in hindsight, quite a bit nostalgic vibe. It set the proper anti-poetry tone for a creative form that was very much in transition. Bukowski felt he knew where the bodies were buried, and was more than willing to lambast his art. In a snippet of dialogue from the finished film, Bukowski was on stun:

"Poetry has always been said to be a private, hidden art. Not to be appreciated. The reason it's not appreciated is because it hasn't shown any guts, hasn't shown any dance. Poetry is generally very dull, very pretentious. Generally, he (the poet) is just a dumb fiddling asshole writing insecure lines that don't come through, believing he is immortal, writing for his immortality that never arrives."

Poetry in Motion, arriving as it did on the heels of the critically less successful *Tales of Ordinary Madness*, was universally praised. A long run in movie houses, followed by years of video, DVD and cable longevity, made this the first feature length film to give poetry its due on a grand scale. And the irony was that it had Bukowski's image and attitude plastered all over it.

The Untold Story of Bukowski the Film Critic

Bukowski moved to San Pedro, California in 1978. He could afford to buy a house. He needed to put some space between himself and his Hollywood roots.

In a sense Bukowski was a San Pedro kind of guy: earthy, hardscrabble, basically salt-of-the-earth. He fit right in to his surroundings. According to a story by Brenda Littleton appearing in the *Cholla Needles Arts and Literary Library*, contrary to his at large image of movie hater, Bukowski would frequent the local Warner Grand movie theater in San Pedro and, in his own Bukowski-like way, offer his opinion.

"Bukowski lived right around the corner from a breakfast café I would frequent," Littleton, a Jungian therapist and author, recalled in her story. "The Grand Warner would show newly released features and Charles Bukowski would go and watch them. I would imagine him sloughed down into the red velvet seats. The next morning he would hang a chalkboard out of his second story window with his rating for the film. Ten was his best rating as was an exclamation point. Most films came in with a three or a four. I always took heed of his critiques. I'd look up (from the restaurant) just to get a glimpse of his hand tossing the chalkboard out the window. I learned to understand his gestures. If he haphazardly threw the chalkboard out the window where it crashed against the side of the building, I knew the rating would be low. If he carefully positioned the board in a quiet way, I knew the rating was going to be high."

Littleton later filled in the blanks in an email interview. "I would park on the same street where he lived, and his window on the second floor would be open. One time I was fortunate enough to be present when he tossed out the chalkboard. We locked eyes for a brief moment and then he ducked inside."

The Killers (1984)

It was a chance meeting in a coffee shop in a poor section of town: a former insurance agent, up to here with the downside of life, and a low level burglar with a plan to get rich quick. They go to Beverly Hills and break into a high-class house. But things don't go as planned. They kill the husband and then rape the wife before cutting her throat, before leaving without anything. End of story.

"The Killers," a short story from the Bukowski collection, *South of No North*, was the writer at his darkest and most primitive. A lot had been made of *The Killers* being an homage to Hemingway, but in Bukowski's hands it was a nasty bit of raw, savage and uncompromising storytelling. And in the hands of German director Patrick Roth, it would become a much talked about and yet seldom seen short film.

The film version of *The Killers*, a 60-minute short with a cast of equally obscure character actors and a couple of fringe name players that include Jack Kehoe, Raymond Mayo, Allan Kolman, Susanne Reed, Anne Ramsey and Susan Tyrrell, is so below the radar that Bukowski seemed to have forgotten about it, save for a couple of short messages between Bukowski and Roth that currently reside in the archives of The Huntington Library thanks to a massive donation of Bukowski memorabilia and ephemera donated by his wife Linda.

Roth approached Bukowski. As always, Bukowski's feeling about the project did not hinge on much more than what was in it for him. Roth offered Bukowski $500 for his services as a co-writer, with Roth, on the script, and for a small cameo, with dialogue, of Bukowski introducing the film while sitting in a railroad boxcar with the words, "Seems like a man has only two choices. Get in on the hustle or become a bum." For the record, Bukowski would be credited in the cast list as "the author but not 'the actor.'"

The Killers was shot in Los Angeles. Roth brought a low budget (reportedly $60,000), minimalist approach that would accentuate the darkness and the disturbing nature of the story. How Bukowski fared as an actor with dialogue is, like just about everything connected with the production, lost in the annals of Bukowski lore. Essentially Bukowski played Bukowski, "the author,"—a part he could do in his sleep. *The Killers* received a miniscule theatrical release beginning in October 1984 in the United States, United Kingdom and Germany under the Patrick Roth Production banner before disappearing. Roth had high hopes for *The Killers*, proclaiming that he was using the film as a pilot for a possible television series in the United States or Europe, but nothing ever came of that venture.

For whatever reason, Roth promptly left the filmmaking business and devoted his energy to novels. In hindsight, Bukowski would praise the film and Roth as only Bukowski could, in a conversation with the *Steigerwald Post*. "I think the kid has a touch of something, and it's not malaria. I didn't like suddenly flashing that guy with his throat cut. It looked like a rubber doll with ketchup. But all in all, I think he hit 91 (out of 100). What the hell more can you ask?"

The Killers, which has been praised for its disturbing content and adherence to Bukowski's original story, also holds the distinction of being the first time that a film of a Bukowski short story was attempted. As Bukowski's reputation continued to grow, it would not be the last.

900 Pounds (1987)

Two out of work and down on their luck authors make the mistake of making fun of two massively obese people in a cheap motel swimming pool. The two fat men take offense and chase down the authors with an intent to kill. Equally pitiful and hilarious in a dark sort of way, *900 Pounds*, a 12-minute short directed by Alan Abrams, exhibits a minimalist, by degrees darkly humorous style to go hand in hand with Bukowski's style of gut-punch storytelling.

900 Pounds is based on a slim, five page short story that appeared in the collection *Hot Water Music* in 1983. Like the original story, *900 Pounds*, budgeted at $12,000, is quick, stark and, within extremely low budget limitations, the perfect distillation of what Bukowski, at his minimalist best, was all about.

Actor Fritz Fox related, with tongue slightly in cheek, his entry into the world of *900 Pounds*. "I was in San Francisco Art Institute at the time, taking film production classes, and a book of Bukowski short stories was brought to me by a filmmaker named Alan Abrams. Abrams offered me a part in this short film he was making."

Fox had read Bukowski and "liked his writing a lot." But he did have some reservations. "When I read the story I was certain that I was being typecast. But I went ahead anyway. While I was preparing for the role, I did, along with the director and the cameraman, a couple of bindles of coke, and drank numerous beers. I thought that was what the part called for, and I wanted to be in character."

Fox was light on anecdotes, but offered, "Overall, the adaptation was good. I liked it. But I felt that I could have been more inspired. I think a couple of more lines of powder could have helped me."

900 Pounds, starring Roy Eisenstein, Fritz Fox and Raye Lynn Jacobs, would suffer the fate of most short films of the day. It was rarely seen, and quickly melted into the realm of obscurity. These days, thanks to the development of the internet and its constant need for product, *900 Pounds* has become more accessible, and is more than worth the 12 minutes it will take out of your day.

Fox speculated on what Bukowski would have thought of the film. "I think Charles would think I should have held out for more drugs and beer."

The Road to Barfly (1979-1986)

Schroeder envisioned *Barfly* as being a small film, big on isolated and often claustrophobic sets and locations. Early on, he envisioned *Barfly* with a very modest $3.5 million budget.

The only stumbling block was that the "money boys" who he would normally approach to fund a movie had no idea who Bukowski was, not surprisingly, and what second hand info they had gleaned indicated that his world was not tied up in a hearts and flowers story. How could a tale of a down and out alcoholic and the people who inhabited that world have any entertainment value, they wanted to know, as their checkbooks disappeared into their pockets. Getting the money was a hard sell.

Casting *Barfly* was a whole other matter. As his fame as an author had grown, Bukowski had suddenly become the darling of the Hollywood set, not the pretty boys but, rather, a rugged new breed of actors, and legendary auteurs like Goddard and Herzog who bucked the system at every opportunity.

Bukowski was both amused and leery when the likes of Sean Penn and Madonna began coming into his world. They were the young actors on the rise. He liked their attitude and, by degrees, their pretense of being worldly and literary. That they kissed his ass and usually brought booze was the icing on the cake. But in his typically Bukowski like fashion, he tended to see some of the biggest names in the film world as borderline contemptible.

"People have come around even before this shit happened," Bukowski recalled in a *Film Comment* interview. "James Woods before he became big time. Through Barbet I met Harry Dean Stanton. Harry Dean's a strange fellow. He just sits around depressed. Sean Penn seemed very withdrawn and delicate. One time I made a remark about Madonna (whom Penn was romantically involved with at the time) which was not flattering. He was sitting right next to me. He started standing up. I said,

'Hey Sean, sit down, you know I can take you, don't be silly.' He sat back down."

Tensions between Bukowski and Penn would usually cool, which, inevitably, lead to discussions about *Barfly*. Penn read the script and enthusiastically offered to play the part of the film's Bukowski alter ego Henry Chinaski—for a dollar. Schroeder and Bukowski were both leery of the offer. Penn at that point had a certain amount of cache in Hollywood that might make funding the film a bit easier. But Penn turned out to be a bit on the pushy side, and Bukowski and Schroeder had already formed an unshakable bond.

Penn persisted and visited Bukowski and Schroeder at the writer's home, fellow actor and director Dennis Hopper in tow, and laid his cards on the table, Bukowski recalled in *Film Comment*. "Penn wanted Dennis Hopper to direct, Barbet would be the producer and Penn would star in the film. It was a pretty lush deal. But I wanted Barbet to direct because he had put seven years into this. Barbet said [to Sean Penn], 'No! I must direct this myself.'"

Bukowski formed an immediate dislike and distrust of Hopper, and Schroeder had a bit of history with Hopper, himself, that was not good. Hopper had once told him that he did not think that Schroeder could direct traffic— uch less direct. After Penn and Hopper left, Bukowski and Schroeder had a good laugh at Hopper's expense before deciding that any deal involving Hopper directing would be dead on arrival.

Bukowski, in *Film Comment*, told a story of Schroeder punctuating his distaste for Hopper in very dramatic fashion. "After the meeting, Barbet got on the phone and changed his will to say 'In case I die, Dennis Hopper is never to be allowed to direct *Barfly*. Anyone else in the world but Dennis Hopper.'"

Without Hopper's involvement, Penn was immediately out of the picture. As the Hollywood gossip mill churned about *Barfly* and Bukowski, a number of other names were floated to play Henry Chinaski. These included James Woods, who was just off an excellent performance in *The Onion Field*, and singer-songwriter Tom Waits, who went so far as to go to Bukowski's home for drinks. If you know anything about Waits, easily one of the closest to the Bukowski attitude and creative outlook, you realize how eventful that conversation must have been. Years later, in a conversation with *The Word* magazine, Waits would recall the night he confronted Bukowski during what had been an alcohol getting-to-know-you at the writer's house.

"You try to match him drink for drink," remembered Waits, "but you're a novice, you're a child and you're drinking with a roaring pirate. So I thought I was able to hang in there, but I wasn't able to. They tried to get me in that movie *Barfly*, playing Bukowski. They offered me a lot of money but I just couldn't do it. I just didn't consider myself a good enough actor."

Singer-songwriter Kris Kristofferson was also in the running for a while. Bukowski, as reported in the book *Locked in the Arms of a Crazy Life*, was upset with the notion that *Barfly* might feature Henry Chinaski singing and playing guitar. As it would turn out, none of the aforementioned would ultimately commit to the film, which played havoc with Schroeder's attempt to get funding.

Then along came Mickey Rourke. Into the mid 1980's the actor had established himself as a raw talent, and a temperamental one at that, often prone to conflicts on set and flashes of unhealthy ego. In the films *Year of the Dragon*, *9½ Weeks* and *Angel Heart* he was being favorably compared to James Dean and Marlon Brando in their prime. Schroeder was high on Rourke, and would tell Bukowski that he had found the ideal actor to play Henry Chinaski. That Rourke had no idea who Bukowski was and had never read any of his work seemed, initially, a minor drawback.

"I hadn't met Mickey, but I had heard many stories about him," Bukowski told *Film Comment*. " I thought 'This guy will be a complete prick. I better not get drunk and take a swing at him. I better watch my drinking. I could ruin the whole movie by getting into it with this kid and being completely honest."

Bukowski and Rourke would finally meet over drinks and feel each other out. To Bukowski's admitted surprise, he said in *Film Comment*, the actor was not so bad after all. "He was so nice. His eyes were good. I think we just liked each other."

With Rourke essentially set in the role of Chinaksi, the search for an actress to play the equally damaged Wanda, a pivotal emotional twist in the *Barfly* story, was on. And as these things often play out in Hollywood, fate would play a definite hand in landing Faye Dunaway.

In her memoir, *Looking for Gatsby*, Dunaway recalled the bite of that casting apple. "My husband, Terry (a photographer) was assigned to take some pictures of Mickey Rourke, and I went with him to meet Mickey. Over dinner [Rourke] began telling me about a new film he had gotten involved in, and [said] there was a meaty role for me if I was interested. Was I ever!"

Dunaway's enthusiasm for the suggestion was not surprising. Since what many considered her high water mark as an actress in *Bonnie and Clyde*, Dunaway had been on a slow but steady decline in casting circles, owing more to her advancing age than to any lack of talent. The film roles she was getting were marginal, and, to add insult to injury, she was more frequently getting offers to do television.

In short order, Dunaway contacted Schroeder with her interest, and was given the script to Barfly. "When I was reading the script, it was like I was talking to you," she told film critic Roger Ebert. "There's usually something phony in a script. This one was so alive, it was coming off the page."

Schroeder almost immediately agreed that Dunaway would be ideal for the role of Wanda, and went to Bukowski with the good news. Bukowski was less than thrilled, based largely on what he thought was a less than stellar performance in *Bonnie and Clyde*. "I saw her in *Bonnie and Clyde*," he stated in *Film Comment,* shortly after the completion of *Barfly*. "She [had] filled her role. Period. She wasn't bad. Sorry to say this, Faye. You want me to lie? I just made an enemy. That's one of my problems. I can't lie." But Schroeder convinced Bukowski that Dunaway was perfect for the role, adding as an aside that her name recognition would help with their still-elusive funding. As for Dunaway, she was candid in her autobiography *Looking for Gatsby* in saying that *Barfly* was a literal lifesaver for her. "The character of Wanda is my way back to the light. This is a role that I care deeply about. I haven't felt this passion for a character since *Network*. I saw the promise of a comeback for me in the agonized face of Wanda."

The rest of the cast slowly fell into place. Helen Hunt had initially been selected to play the tough as nails publishing house maven Tully Sorenson, but was replaced by Alice Krige when Schroeder felt that the character required an actress with more experience. It would be Rourke's insistence that his good buddy Frank Stallone have the part as the bartender who locks horns with Henry.

With the first rate cast now in place, funding for the film had suddenly kicked into high gear, and one of the frontrunners for the project was Cannon Films, the notorious run and gun dealmakers known for going the extra mile to get the money and a picture made. But by late 1986 Cannon Films had fallen on hard times. A string of less than successful films had suddenly made investors gun-shy when it came to rolling the dice with Cannon. Suddenly turned what had looked like a sure bet with *Barfly* and Cannon had disintegrated into a flat out rejection of the project.

Bukowski was disappointed. Schroeder was frantic at the Cannon dismissal. And, in a story that even by Hollywood standards was almost too outrageous to believe, Schroeder stormed into the offices of Cannon's CEO's and actually threatened bloody violence, according to an interview Bukowski did with film critic *Roger Ebert.com*.

"Barbet had been trying to make this movie for seven years. A few months earlier it looked like Cannon was about to cancel the film. Barbet goes to the office of Menahem Golan, the president of Cannon, with an electric handsaw. He pulls out a syringe of Novacaine and shoots it into his little finger. He says he will cut off his little finger if Menahem doesn't make the movie, and that he will continue to cut off parts of his body and send them to Menahem until he agrees to make the movie. Menahem tells him to go to hell. Barbet plugs in the handsaw."

Schroeder would admit, years later, that it was just as much publicity stunt as it was a real threat. But the effort to make *Barfly* had turned into an almost military campaign in which there was a lot at stake. Dunaway, sitting on the sidelines as her big career comeback was sinking fast, would take matters into her own hands, she recalled in her memoir *Looking for Gatsby*.

"It is early 1987 and I have fought like a wildcat to keep this project alive. One weekend I stayed on the phone for hours, talking to anyone who would listen, including the head of a French bank and a couple of producers I knew. I refused to stop pressuring them (Cannon Films). I had a fairly good sense of what they needed to make this happen."

Dunaway understood how Hollywood worked, and so she knew that the bottom line would always be money. And as she would recall in her memoir, money was a card she was more than willing to play. "I made the final offer for a deal that Cannon could not refuse. I offered to work for no money upfront and to forego my salary in exchange for a deferment or a percentage of the profits. With that offer Cannon found the money somewhere and gave Barbet his deal.

"Usually you celebrate when a movie production wraps. We celebrated the first day of the production, a day that almost had not come."

Charles Bukowski's Give Me Your Love (1986)

Charles Bukowski's Give Me Your Love is a film so shrouded in obscurity and, yes, a small amount of mystery that it's amazing. But here it is and here goes:

The first of several attempts at interpreting Bukowski's tragi/comedy about a man and woman and infidelity centered around a psychiatric institute—a story whose origin was as a in a small one-story chapbook illustrated by R. Crumb in 1983.

We know this much. It was a UCLA student film. It was shot in a day, on a soundstage, by a director named Jamie Campo, a pseudonym for a director who, to this day, remains unknown. It starred a young Taiwanese actor named Conrad Hurtt, uncredited in the film.

Hurtt, as of 2023 a teacher in the Los Angeles Unified School District, expressed surprise at being "rediscovered" after 35 years when we was approached for an interview. In conversation with this author as he attempted to unravel the inconsistencies of the 6:40 truncated version of Bukowski's original story. "Jamie Campo was not the name of the director. I have no record of the director's real name. He used that name. Jamie had directed me in a different project and I needed a director's name for the IMDB website. All I know about the real director is that he was a UCLA film student. The reason I was uncredited in the film was, I assume, because the filmmaker had no budget for credits."

The only thing Hurtt knew about Bukowski at the time was that the movie *Barfly* was about to come out. He had not read any of Bukowski's work, but, upon reading the script for *Give Me Your Love*, he was duly impressed. "I thought it was funny. The filmmakers had a really good sense of humor and really gave us free reign in a creative way."

To call the production "shoestring" was an understatement. A minimal set consisting of two plywood walls, a cot and a chair were set up in a soundstage on the UCLA campus. The dialogue-heavy, one-day

71

shoot was amateurish in execution, but strangely spirited by film student standards, and, according to Hurtt, it finished on time and on budget. Fragmentary accounts indicated that *Charles Bukowski's Give Me Your Love* was seen in public only once, at a one-time screening in a theater on the UCLA campus, before disappearing into obscurity only to occasionally appear on a handful of YouTube channels.

Hurtt received a VHS copy of the film for his efforts, and, years later, posted it himself on YouTube. He moved on from an acting career consisting of bit parts and extra roles to a career in teaching. Looking back, Hurtt acknowledged, "I loved the film," but eventually decided to take *Charles Bukowski's Give Me Your Love* down from the internet. "Because of the foul language, I removed it from YouTube. I'm a high school teacher now and I didn't want my students having access to me saying curse words on their smartphones."

BARFLY (1987)

As *Barfly* was preparing to begin filming in February, 1987, the question of what Hollywood would do to Charles Bukowski, his life and times, was once again front and center. Yes, Bukowski had written the screenplay his way, and Schroeder swore on a stack of proverbial Bibles that even the minutest question would have to be okayed by the screenwriter. In 1979, in an *L.A. Weekly* story, Schroeder, bordering on downright humble, confessed, "I was astonished at having gotten Bukowski to do this. It will be as much his [Bukowski's] film as it is mine."

But for hardcore followers of Bukowski, the question remained: would Hollywood do right by *Barfly,* or would they screw it up? Bukowski, ever the cynic about just about everything, was caught up in the moment and surprisingly upbeat when he gave *Barfly*, his blessing during an on set interview with film critic Roger Ebert. "The movie is called *Barfly*, and it's about me because that's what I was, a *Barfly*. You ran errands for sadists and let the bartender beat you up because you were the bar clown. You filled people's days with your presence and maybe you'd get a few free drinks now and then."

Bukowski would be understated and ironic as he assessed the chances for *Barfly* in an interview with the magazine *Twisted Image*. "If the actors can say their lines right, this could be a pretty fair movie."

Any doubts that Bukowski had about *Barfly* being anything but an authentic representation of his life were quickly assuaged. Schroeder had been as good as his word. He was shooting *Barfly* exactly as Bukowski had written it. If there were minor quibbles on dialogue, Schroeder would immediately go to Bukowski, who would either fix them himself or suggest changes. Cinematically, *Barfly* seemed spot on. The lion's share of *Barfly* was shot in two Los Angeles dive bars—the kind of places Bukowski had frequented. The realism extended to Schroeder hiring real regulars at these bars—Barflys themselves—as extras. After filming was completed, with the tip courtesy of Bukowski himself, is was discovered that the apartment building where Wanda's apartment was located was the actual building where Bukowski and his lover Jane Baker Cooney had lived.

Perhaps most importantly to Bukowski's sense of ease on this project, was the open invitation Schroeder extended to Bukowski to come down to the set and hang out anytime he wanted. It was an invitation that Bukowski readily accepted.

On those days when Bukowski did venture down to various *Barfly* sets, he found a cinematic mirror of his world looking back at him. The locations were set up spot-on accurate reflections of the places where Bukowski had literally spent his entire life. The cast: Alice Krige, Frank Stallone, and Jack Nance and other character actors' well-nuanced performances offered up the light and shadow of the author's world. Nothing is perfect, but suffice it to say, Schroeder had done his homework.

The mutual admiration society that had developed between Bukowski and Rourke only deepened on the first day of filming when, Bukowski, who was already caught up in the excitement of playing the Hollywood game, decided to show up on the very first day of filming. As soon as Rourke spotted Bukowski, he invited him over to his trailer for a shot of whisky before filming began. He then told Bukowski that he was welcome to stop by the set and stay as long as he liked. As chronicled in the book *Locked in the Arms of a Crazy Life*, Bukowski's response was "Okay. I'll Stay Forever."

In fact, Bukowski would be a regular visitor to the set of *Barfly*, sometimes with his wife Linda, and filming would literally come to a halt when they saw Bukowski rambling onto the set. Bukowski would be mild mannered, often to the point of being gentle, soft spoken and accommodating to those around him. Cast and crew members would gather around him, fawning and paying tribute to the man who was a grizzled old rock star basking in the glory that was his life coming to film.

Bukowski was nothing if not amenable during his days on the *Barfly* set. If director Schroeder or any of the actors had a question about a line of dialogue, he was quick to clarify or, on several occasions, change the line on the spot. One day, when Faye Dunaway was scheduled to shoot a scene, she came over to Bukowski, notebook in hand, and peppered him with questions relating to Wanda, her character. Bukowski would also be pressed into service as a stand in for Mickey Rourke during the rehearsal of the scene, and even played to type as a barfly in the scene where Henry meets Wanda for the first time.

His time on the set afforded Bukowski the opportunity to observe Rourke and Dunaway at length. Ever the critic, Bukowski could never get past the "Okay, but nothing special," when it came to Dunaway. When it came to Rourke, it would be a whole other matter, as he recalled in *Film Comment*. "The guy was great. He really became this barfly. He added his own dimension. At first I thought 'this is awful. He's overdoing it.' As the shooting went on, I saw he had done the right thing. He had created a very strange, fantastic, loveable character."

With the completion of principle photography, Bukowski had time to sit back and reflect on this Hollywood experience. But with the passage of time, his attitude toward the acting mutated from laudatory to super critical.

In a letter to Teresa Leo in 1992, published in the collection *Reach for the Sun: Selected Letters 1978-1994*, Bukowski maliciously slammed the film, saying, "I preferred Sean Penn to Mickey Rourke, but Sean wanted his own director, and we had to stick with Barbet Schroeder, so that didn't work out. Sean is a much better actor. Faye Dunaway? Well I think we could have done better. She really didn't play it insane enough."

Bukowski was downright charitable to Dunaway when compared to the sudden attacks he leveled against Rourke which are chronicled for posterity in the documentary *Born into This*. "Rourke didn't get it right. He had it all kind of exaggerated, untrue. He was a little bit show off about it. He overdid it."

In hindsight, Rourke's remarks about the experience, archived in *Bukowski Quotes.com*, were catty about almost everyone involved. "Bukowski was okay for a drunk. Schroeder was a self-centered prick and an asshole."

Bukowski was privy to the early rough cuts of *Barfly* during the editing stage, and, in a 1992 letter to Teresa Leo from the collection *Reach for the Sun*, he was resigned to what he saw as the finished film. "I had very little input once the film got going. Some of the scenes I didn't think fit the reality enough, others worked. But to hell with the writer. It's just his baby. All in all though, I'm glad the film was made." And truth be known, Bukowski's ego, all complaints aside, was tickled by the process of a full blown, fairly big budget motion picture being made of his life. In fact, for a period, he would tell anyone who would listen that *Barfly* would most certainly get Academy Award nominations.

Bukowski was still flush with excitement upon the film's completion, and, accordingly, agreed to make himself available for interviews as part of the *Barfly* publicity campaign. He did an interview with Sean Penn that was published by *People* magazine, but said "Thanks, but no thanks" to a request to appear on *The Johnny Carson Show*. He was the media darling of the moment, and was constantly bombarded with questions designed to go for the easy hook: Boozehound Makes Good. By the time *Barfly* had its premiere showing, complete with a glitzy Hollywood party, Bukowski's love affair with *Barfly* was pretty much over. Bukowski drank quite heavily at the afterparty and, according to the biography *Locked in the Arms of a Crazy Life*, this brief love affair with Hollywood finally came to its inevitable end.

"I've got to get out of here," he told his wife Linda at one point. "This place stinks! It's making me sick!"

Barfly was released on October 16, 1987 and, no pun intended, the film was given the bum rush by Cannon. Released in two theaters domestically, the film suffered critically from those who either did not get it or were inclined to not like it because of they objected to the idea that a less than desirable personality would get a movie made of his miscreant life. Reviews were mixed at best. The box office was slim, and it would take the not surprising success of *Barfly* in Europe, where Bukowski had long been considered God, to get the movie slightly past its break-even point.

How much of an impact *Barfly* would have on Bukowski's heretofore underground reputation is open to conjecture, according to Bukowski book editor and academic Abel Debritto. "*Barfly* boosted book sales quite substantially. All of a sudden this dirty old man very few Americans were truly aware of was being interviewed by *People* magazine, the tabloids and the movie magazines. I don't think his reputation changed that much. I think *Barfly* made him more popular for a while. But Bukowski had been well known on the small press scene for almost 20 years when *Barfly* was released. He already had a reputation all over the world. *Barfly* kind of glorified something that was already there."

Critics aside, when the dust settled, *Barfly* had done its job of catapulting Bukowski up from the underground and into some small level of polite commercial society. Or at the very least, it had created him as a rather unorthodox flavor of the moment.

The Charles Bukowski Tapes (1987)

Despite Bukowski's snarling, combative face that he showed to prying eyes, there are two elements of his character that are often overlooked: he was a man who loved his solitude, and he was very loyal to those he let into that solitary world. It was this side of Bukowski that would lead to the creation of *The Charles Bukowski Tapes*, the mammoth four-hour up-close and personal look at Bukowski the man, the writer and someone fully capable of saying both outlandish and profound things. *The Charles Bukowski Tapes* is a series of 52 interviews (broken down into bite sized segments of two to 10 minutes), culled from 64 hours of raw interview footage of Bukowski pontificating on everything connected to his world and beyond.

During an interview with *Film Comment*, Bukowski explained the odyssey that became *The Charles Bukowski Tapes* which began with the seven-year battle to get *Barfly* made. "I had a guilt complex because I never thought Barbet would get *Barfly* off the ground. One night Barbet had the thought that he would get me drunk and I would talk into a video camera."

As it turned out, Schroeder, when he was not beating his head against the wall trying to get investors for *Barfly*, was spending a lot of time with Bukowski, getting drunk and marveling at how the poet could talk about any subject for any length of time. As he would recount at various points with the *New York Times* and in the press kit for *The Charles Bukowski Tapes*, he was deeply enamored of the man.

"Born of what I called my frustration that nobody wanted to make the film [*Barfly*], I thought, 'Here I am spending evenings with this extraordinary man. I'm having so much fun. Why should I be the only one?' I could not stand the thought of not sharing the extraordinary evenings we spent with this man."

It would not take long for Schroeder, who always seemed to see the cinematic possibilities in everything, to come up with a plan. "I finally brought in a small crew, friends of mine, with a high quality video setup. If we had one rule, it was the least drunk person in the room took control of the camera. I've never liked formal interviews. I tried to get him started on a topic and then just keep from interrupting him."

Most of what would be an estimated 62 hours of filming would be done in Bukowski and then girlfriend—soon to be wife—Linda Lee's San Pedro home. There would also be occasional forays into Bukowski's old neighborhood haunts, including the house where Bukowski grew up. Bukowski, again feeling guilty at the healthy amount of money he had received upfront for the *Barfly* script that was now going nowhere, and also a bit amused and intrigued at the prospect of being the subject of an up-close and personal documentary that could seemingly go on forever, was more than happy to oblige.

"I got drunk for many days, many hours and many hours and talked with the camera on me," he related in a letter to poet Gerald Locklin that appeared in the collection *Reach for the Sun*. "I think I babbled pretty lucky and pretty wild."

Over the course of filming, Bukowski, often after a few drinks, was the ideal foil, going on at length about sex, violence, women, drinking, his life growing up and all manner of topics. Bukowski was the ringmaster in a non-stop examination of his attitudes and psyche, and through the chaos that inevitably ensued, he was probing deep into his own id and ego. It was quickly turning into something raw, primitive and real—as only Bukowski could present it. But it was an examination that would occasionally come at a price.

Whether by choice or chance, we see Bukowski at his most humane and vulnerable when he is leading the camera crew through the dark days of his childhood as the memories of childhood abuse surface during a tour of his childhood home and a visit to the bathroom where he was beaten on a regular basis by his father. "Here we have the torture chamber," Bukowski sadly enlightened the camera crew. This is the torture chamber where I learned something. I don't know, it's just a terrible place to stand and talk about it. You don't want to talk about it too much. Let's just forget it."

Throughout the days and hours of filming, Bukowski was all over the place: melancholy, sad, petulant and angry, depending on his mood at the moment and the amount of alcohol he had been drinking. One day of excessive drinking, a mood, with the hours, was turning violent. Linda had been out during the day and, upon returning home, it was obvious that she had been drinking as well. The fuse was lit when Bukowski let loose with a diatribe about how women have used and abused him. Linda prodded him by saying that he let those things happen to him. Bukowski got angry, and, in a profanity-laden attack, accused Linda of going out at all hours and cheating on him.

The back and forth tirade between Linda and Bukowski continued to escalate as the camera continued to roll… right up to the moment when Bukowski completely lost it, kicking Linda and taking a swing at her. The next morning, Bukowski claimed he had no memory of the altercation the night before. Linda would, in quotes chronicled in the biography *Locked in the Arms of a Crazy Life*, go to great lengths to smooth over what had happened.

"I remember thinking afterwards, everybody is going to think that this is the way we live our life, he beats me and this and that. I swear he never had before, and he never did again."

The Charles Bukowski Tapes was released to much interest and speculation. To longtime observers of Bukowski, the documentary/docudrama was a milestone of sorts, capturing the essence of who Charles Bukowski was. And it was a detailed look at what guided him through his life. It was as if Schroeder was the bullfighter, waving the camera/cape in front of Bukowski the bull, in hopes of drawing blood. Others thought the *Tapes* a bit contrived and a bit exploitive.

The Charles Bukowski Tapes continue to be an important relic of the man and his life, and are easily the high water mark for those who have attempted to get at the heart of Bukowski through cinema. Bukowski had his own response to *The Tapes*:

"I liked them (the film) the first time I saw them," he reflected in a *Film Comment* interview. "The second time it was just an old drunk talking away."

Crazy Love(1987)

In the universe of Charles Bukowski cinema, *Crazy Love* a/k/a *Love is a Dog from Hell* may well be the most sensitive look at the author. In the hands of director Dominque Deruddere, it is also a most challenging, artsy film. It is alternately morose and humorous, and in a quite surreal manner it probes the realities of youthful desire, love and loneliness. Many in darker critical circles have suggested that *Crazy Love*, with its attention to sex and body horror, necrophilia and voyeurism, was a very David Cronenberg kind of movie, and one that many critics were quick to acknowledge as one of the best films of the 80's.

Bukowski, on the occasion of having seen the film, praised the effort, in an interview with *Beat Scene Magazine*. "I liked *Crazy Love*. As I told Deruddere, 'You made me look better than I am.' He over sensitized me. But it came out nicely and much of it was actually me."

Crazy Love is a three-part odyssey spanning the life of a man named Harry who pursues his unrequited passions surrounding love and sex through several decades of lust and longing. As a young boy, Harry is consumed with love fantasies surrounding princesses and happy endings as only a nine year old can conceive of them. As a teen with disfiguring facial acne, Harry suffers the rigors of being a social outcast and a pariah in the world of teen sexuality and love. Finally, as a down and out loner, he finds himself suddenly given over to an outrageous and taboo love relationship that ends, romantically and tragically in his... well there will be no spoiler here. *Crazy Love* is a movie rich in humor, sadness, tragedy and, in the finest art house tradition, an ending that offers up both redemption and fulfillment in a surreal manner. It is easy to see why Bukowski fell all over himself in praising the work.

As with seemingly every Bukowski film effort, *Crazy Love's* origin is full of creative and emotional slight of hand and ingenuity. In 1985, director Deruddere was a relatively unknown Belgian director, contemplating his first major creative effort. Having discovered the power of Bukowski, Deruddere found inspiration in the author's story *The Copulating Mermaid of Venice, California* for his first short film of any consequence, entitled *A Foggy Night*. About the time Deruddere was contemplating creating *A Foggy Night*, he was also negotiating funding with the Flemish Film Commission for another Bukowski story, *The Great Zen Wedding*, for which he had applied for and had received a grant to make.

As reported on *Bukowski Forum.com*, it was about that time that the director read *The Copulating Mermaid of Venice, California* and had decided that was the story he wanted to make. Playing fast and loose with the funding, Deruddere, without mentioning his change of mind, went ahead with *A Foggy Night,* literally under the nose of the film commission who, upon seeing that film, truly believed the director when he insisted that there had been some creative changes to the script, and that *A Foggy Night* was really *The Great Zen Wedding*.

Deruddere was quite content with his completed film, but his creative instincts told him that what he had created was a great third act. He knew he wanted to transform *A Foggy Night* into a full-blown feature that would require additional stories. It was at that point that did what previous filmmakers with Bukowski on the brain would do. He decided to meet his maker.

In *Horror News.net*, it was reported that Deruddere was well aware of Bukowski's dislike for film in general, and had a very public dislike for *Tales of Ordinary Madness*. The director became obsessed with the notion that, for his film to succeed, he would have to get Bukowski's blessing. Deruddere, *A Foggy Night* in hand, travelled to Los Angeles to meet with Bukowski, make his pitch and show him *A Foggy Night*. Bukowski was used to this kind of approach. It appealed to his sense of ego and curiosity. After *Tales of Ordinary Madness*, he was not expecting much, but he was quite impressed with *A Foggy Night* and gave his support to turn it into a feature, going so far as to say that "the short was much better than [his] original story."

Deruddere was so encouraged that he took Bukowski's blessing as a sign that he should go further into Bukowski's creative oeuvre, and he subsequently fashioned the first and second elements of *Crazy Love* out of the incidents described in the book *Ham on Rye*.

Deruddere's cast consisted of a mixture of several veterans of

European art and mainstream film, with the likes of Josse De Pauw, Michael Pas, Amid Chakir, Geert Hunaerts and Florence Beliard more than capable of adding the subtlety and proper shading to the darker and more morose moments of the story. *Crazy Love's* ambitious take found immediate favor internationally, and would have the distinction of being the first Flemish/Belgian film to get a theatrical release in America.

Crazy Love a/k/a *Love is a Dog from Hell*, released sporadically— as most art house films were in Europe and the United States— had critics and serious film observers choosing up sides. *Crazy Love* would not only test the endurance of jaded critics, but also of art house and foreign film fans who were usually more than willing to give any daring voice a chance. The quality of the cinematography, set design and acting received a resounding thumbs up and was enthusiastically championed by the celebrities, including Sean Penn, Madonna and Francis Ford Coppola. But the "in your face" approach of *Crazy Love's* daring subject matter, and the graphic displays of taboo situations made the film an immediate commercial liability that did not attract a large audience. Nevertheless, there was just something about *Crazy Love* that had settled in the mind of the film community intelligentsia and that would just not go away. Word of mouth carried the film for the three years following its release, and would, in years to come, become considered an underground classic. Today, in many circles, it is considered one of the most influential films of the 80's.

In the film world Bukowski was now being considered high art and, yes, something special.

Lune Froide (1988) and Lune Froide/Cold Moon (1991)

The notion presented by Bukowski of the taboo subject of necrophilia, as depicted in his short story *The Copulating Mermaid of Venice California*, would continue to have its way with Europe's more daring filmmakers well into the 80's and 90's. One of the least known but critically acclaimed adaptations was the 1988 short film *Lune Froide*, in which two down on their luck alcoholics steal a corpse out of a parked mortuary truck that turns out to be an attractive dead woman. After one of the drunks violates the dead woman, she is carried out into the sea where she is given a drunken burial. The film incorporated two Bukowski stories: *The Copulating Mermaid of Venice California.* and *Trouble with the Battery*, and featured Patrick Bouchitey doing double duty as director and actor, and a small cast that included Karine Nuris and Jean Francois Stevenin.

The black and white 26-minute short, *Lune Froide*, was directed by the legendary—at least in more fringe circles—French director Bouchitey. It was shot on a shoestring budget and recorded in mono sound, all the better to maximize Bouchitey's sense of dark romance and horror. For the director, in conversation with *Chroniques Des Fontaines*, it was an important film, to his way of thinking.

"For me, it is important because it is a completely unconscious film. I wondered why I was attracted to the [stories of] Bukowski. This dead woman, this offered woman, this corpse, this image which lived, I found that visual. I found that it had the tunes of a very bizarre tale. A kind of poetry from the garbage cans."

Lune Froide was released briefly in France, and can be found internationally. If one is a Bukowski film completist, this nugget might well be worth the search.

Lune Froide had an expanded second incarnation in 1991. While the original short was gathering awards and interest in Europe, it came to the attention of producer/director Luc Besson, who encouraged Bouchitey to expand the concept and storyline into a full length feature.

With a bigger budget and longer shooting schedule, Bouchitey would bring in a bigger ensemble of actors that included himself, Nuris and Stevenin from the short, and newcomers Jean Pierre Besson, Conseulo De Haviland, Laura Favali, Silvanna De Faria, Roland Blanche, Jean Pierre Castaldi, Dominique Maurin, Bernard Crombey, Patrick Fierry, Anne Macina, Marie Mergey, Emanuelle Beraud Dufour, Jackie Berroyer, Pierre Bouchette and Perrick Charpentier.

The director was not about to let the short go to waste, and the 92-minute running time of what would be christened *Cold Moon* would include a backstory and would use 26 minutes of the original short. The full-length version allowed for a deeper sense of tension, irony and character depth, while remaining true to Bukowski's work.

Love Pig a/k/a Bring Me Your Love (1990)

Academy Award-winning editor Chris Innis (*The Hurt Locker*) had never met Bukowski. At least she didn't think so.

"I never did meet Bukowski that I am aware of," she said. "Although I always felt he could have been lurking on a bar seat nearby, or that I could have easily passed him on the street. It would have been great to meet Bukowski."

But while she had never met the author face to face, she had read his stories while at the University Of Berkeley as a student in the Independent Film Studies program at Cal Arts, while juggling a day job as production and post production coordinator on the television series *America's Funniest Home Videos.* and had grown fond of the movie *Barfly*. In a creative sense, Innis felt she knew him very well. "I was attracted to the honesty and grittiness of Bukowski's writing. It was unapologetic, and yet romanticized the writers'/artists' lifestyle."

Innis had been particularly enamored, in a cinematic sense, of the short story *Give Me Your Love*, a claustrophobic tale of lust and unfaithfulness centered around a husband, wife and a mental institution, and was contemplating making the tiny tale into an equally miniscule movie. "I had been a fan of Charles Bukowski's work. I had read 'Give Me Your Love' and I liked it. It had crazy, paranoid characters, and was limited to two locations. I thought it would be just the right length for a short film."

Innis recruited her cast and crew from her Cal Arts circle of friends and acquaintances with the promise of lots of laughs and class credit for independent study. *Give Me Your Love* was low budget in the extreme, replete with non actors. But Innis, a real student of detail at that point in her career, would go to great lengths to get even the small moments right.

"Prior to filming, I went to Bukowski's old neighborhood in Hollywood near Western and Hollywood and picked up a business card from one of the seedy hotels in the area, *The Bon Air*. The business card from the seedy hotel would be a real prop in the film, where the main character needed to give another character a number to call and something to stick in his shoe later."

It soon became evident that Innis's *Give Me Your Love* would be limited, in its casting options, to rank amateurs. But her non-actors turned out to be a blessing in disguise. She discovered that they were, by degrees, natural actors, and perhaps more importantly, always available. Plus they never complained and were easy to work with.

For Innis, who only had one previous directorial short under her belt, *Give Me Your Love*—which she decided to rename *Love Pig* when a twinge of possible copyright infringement hit—was admittedly a project of trial and error. In hindsight, Innis recalled that a big mistake was giving her non-actors line readings that resulted in what she called, "A non-heavy handed, kitschy, winky cadence in keeping with the style of a John Waters film." She continued, "I hear that now when I rewatch the film and it makes me cringe."

Innis gathered her cast from a pool of fellow film school students: Nick Szeggda, Christine Chang, Betty Burkhart and William Jones, but flipped the switch when it came to the characters Bukowski had crafted. "I switched the gender of all the roles to sort of make it more female centric. In the original story, it is the woman who is paranoid that she is being cheated on. So I switched it to the man and made the doctor female and Asian. The film gave the women the more dominantly male roles."

Innis was also learning on the fly about the fine art of editing, which would, years later, make her an Academy Award winner. "I'm very embarrassed about some of the cuts I made, and it's one reason I rarely show the film. It feels very raw and amateurish, and the language in the film is also intentionally very crude. I was trying to be a bit vulgar and shocking."

Innis had pretty much kept the production of *Give Me Your Love* below the radar, but during what she deemed a pivotal scene in the film, she was inspired to go public. "I wanted to use the raunchy rap song 'Me So Horny' by *2 Live Crew*. So I wrote Luther Campbell, the leader of the group, a passionate letter about free speech and how I did not intend to profit from it, and I was surprised when he gave me permission. That's the song that ends up being played during the scene with the couple going at it. It's a bit over the top but I like it."

With *Give Me Your Love* a/k/a *Love Pig* completed and well into the editing stage, Innis began having second thoughts about the legal ramifications of using the Bukowski story without his permission. "I didn't worry about getting the film rights or permission to film it, because it would only be seen in a film class, or maybe at film festivals if I were lucky. I didn't expect to make any money from it. It was just going to be a film exercise. I also thought that renaming the film *Love Pig* might have solved the rights issue."

But Innis recalled that she had a change of mind regarding the legal aspects of what she had already done. "As I was editing it, I realized the mistake I had made and decided to reach out to Charles Bukowski to try and get permission after the fact. I had nothing to lose. Well, actually I did risk that he or his publisher could try and stop the project which could have really sucked. But I was young and naïve, and I also knew I wasn't important enough for them to get too bothered about."

Or so she thought.

"So I wrote to Bukowski via his publisher Black Sparrow Press. I didn't hear back from Bukowski, but his publisher wrote back and was very angry with me for not having contacted him in advance. He said the rights to *Give Me Your Love* had already been optioned to somebody named Star Sutherland. I wrote to Star and told him that I was only interested in nonexclusive rights and not for profit purposes and Star wrote back and granted permission."

The completed *Love Pig/Give Me Your Love* was 14 minutes. Innis felt that her film school effort was quite good, but she would remain cautious with the completed film going public. "The initial audience reaction, which was mostly film students at a short film screening, was good. People seemed to like it, laughing and enjoying themselves during the screening, though I think there was some drinking involved. It also played at a few film festivals."

To this day, *Love Pigs/Give Me Your Love* remains a largely unknown addition to the Bukowski film universe. And Innis, all these years later, remains somewhat reticent about taking this missing link public.

"Right now, I'm the only one with copies of the film. I haven't released the film digitally or, for that matter, released it in any way. I'm not sure the world is ready for that, nor am I. Especially now that I have an Oscar-winning image to protect."

The Best Hotel on Skid Row (1990)

Having Bukowski narrate this 1990 HBO documentary *The Best Hotel on Skid Row* was, at first look, a nifty bit of stunt casting. While Bukowski was not physically in this look at the denizens of *The Madison Hotel* that included drug addicts, alcoholics, prostitutes and people hanging onto life by their fingernails, it was a true reflection of what Bukowski has been, and what he writes about. There's an air of authenticity in the haggard tones with which Bukowski describes the life and the characters who are, to a large extent, him and his life.

"We used to go down to skid row for fun, like a break," Bukowski recalled in *Alternative Reel.com*. "Now, for the people down there, there is no way back."

The documentary was directed by Christine Choy, Renee Tajima Pena and Geof Bartz, who reportedly prepped for the film by reading all of Bukowski's books. It is a sad and unsettling 48-minute dark journey into the underside of society. That Bukowski would narrate *The Best Hotel on Skid Row* at a time when all the horrors were largely behind him is a curiosity that he answered in conversation with *The Village Voice.* "I did it for the money, especially when I found out the subject matter. You know, being an ex bum and having lived on skid row, I just fell into it. They said they needed a narrator and I said okay."

All Women Are Named Kiki (1991)

All Women Are Named Kiki, also known in Europe as *Sve Zene Se Zovo Kiki*, was a very early 23 minute long student film by Serbian filmmaker Srdjan Dragojevic, that, reportedly was based on a Charles Bukowski short story of a man who has been in his apartment ever since his wife left him, and gets drunk every night and calls a hot line girl named Kiki.

Little is known of *All Women Are Named Kiki*. Dragojevic drew from a primarily Serbian acting pool. Actors Slabodan Custic, Uros Djuric, Eva Ras and Olivera Jezina would go on to have considerable careers in Europe.

Which Bukowski tale inspired the film is lost in the mists of time, and students of Dragojevic note that the politically-charged filmmaker and author would go on to bigger and better things. But way back in his formative years, he was inspired by the master.

Guts (1991)

"Like anybody can tell you, I am not a very nice man. I don't know the word. I have always admired the villain, the outlaw, the son of a bitch. I like desperate men, men with broken teeth, broken minds and broken ways. They interest me. They are full of surprises and explosions. I'm more interested in perverts than saints. I can relax with bums because I am a bum. I don't like laws, morals, religions, rules. I don't like to be shaped by society."

There you have it: the Bukowski manifesto/philosophy all wrapped up in an excerpt from the introduction to his short story *Guts* which appeared in his *Notes of a Dirty Old Man* column in the *Los Angeles Free Press* on December 10, 1972, and as part of his collection *South of No North* which was published by *Black Sparrow Press* in 1973. *Guts* is the Bukowski ethos personified, showcasing his true, darkly humorous and ironic mercenary, predatory and—dare we acknowledge it—sexist ways, while being more than capable of dealing with life on his own terms. By the 70's, *Guts* and, by association, Bukowski's emotional and character edifice, were set in stone.

Bukowski's down and out hero commiserates with an equal down and outer in a flophouse. He listens somewhat intently as his drinking buddy pines for the affections of a mysterious woman who is living in the basement of the flop house. After a time, the drinking buddy leaves, and our anti-hero makes his way to the basement where he encounters the woman of his friend's desires, and has sex with her. He returns to his apartment, and later discovers that the woman in the basement has suddenly disappeared. End of story.

It would be a story that inspired up and coming Greek filmmaker Yannis Fagras, fresh out of film school and making his way in New York City. He conceived of a 14-minute short, with the aid of actors Jane Frazer (in her one and only acting role before making a career as a producer), John Juback and Alex Murphy.

Murphy recalled, "I was a young actor in New York looking for that all important 'camera time,' when I came across a casting notice from Yannis (director Yannis Fagras) for a student film project. Doing young student filmmaker projects was a real roll of the dice back then just as it is now, and I was not surprised that about 30-50 actors showed up for the auditions. I was lucky to find Yannis' project because I could tell immediately that he was organized, and I felt that he was going to do something with soul."

Murphy felt he had a leg up in landing *Guts* because he was already a bit of a Bukowskiphile. "I had already read some Bukowski by that time and was smitten. I saw that he was a writer who was capable of comedy and tragedy."

And Murphy, who played the Chinaski alter ego on the make in *Guts*, found the ideal foil for a Bukowski film in Fargas. "Yannis was a cool, steady cat. Yannis possibly understood and, more importantly, appreciated more than any American, the virtues of Bukowski's very singular free thinking, his individualism and his literary quest to puke up the naked truth day after day."

As filming began on *Guts*, Murphy quickly grew to appreciate Fargas' approach to directing actors: a free, easy and interpretive style that gave Murphy room to move when it came to playing the Bukowski type. "I was mostly working at trying to get that three o'clock in the morning, slightly sloppy and boozy, loose look and quality in each moment of the scenes, without overdoing it."

Murphy recalled that like all good short films, the *Guts* ensemble succeeded in making magic with little in the way of resources. "Given the limited raw film footage, the bare bones budget and limited time we had, getting it played and shot it did render a good sense of the short story. I liked how we did it. I was a Clash fan, musically, and so I was just happy to play in something with rough edges in both spirit and construction."

The consensus was that Fagras' film was a literal and quite compact distillation of the Bukowski story, with competent performances and all the flaws of a rough, raw filmmaker doing good with rough and raw source material.

Guts would be the latest in a seemingly endless series of short adaptations, first screened on November 8, 1991. It gathered some good reviews and a couple of international film festival awards before disappearing into that void of attempts at bringing Bukowski and his world to cinematic life.

But in looking back on *Guts*, Murphy is unabashedly positive and nostalgic in praise of Bukowski the man. "As I've grown older I find Bukowski even more wise, heartbreaking, honest, funny and, above all, human. When I drop dead I hope there is at least one of Bukowski's books on the kitchen table for somebody to find."

Lonely at the Top (1993) and The Blanket (1994)

At first blush, Bukowski was not your prototypical horror writer. But from the perspective of creating menace and unease, the dirty old man was very much of that genre, especially in psychological construction. One need look no deeper than the story It's *Lonely at the Top* to see how Bukowski figured in the area of shocks and frights.

The set up is the unease that plays in the psyche of even the most formidable individuals that happens when a big dog meets up with an even bigger dog. In this case, it's when the world's most proficient hit man meets up with the biggest, baddest big boss in recent memory.

Budding Chicago filmmaker Gary Mrowca saw the potential of what would turn out to be a come-to-Jesus moment between two characters: Mr. Longo and super hit man Marty, aided slightly by Longo's whipped assistant Percy. It is an emotionally taxing 14 minutes, with an expected ending, but then with a twist on top of that. The actors: Turk Muller, Anthony Cannata and Tony Dicosola, were all effective performers who played things big and broad but were nevertheless effective. Essentially a calling card project, *Lonely at the Top*, distributed on a shoestring by Subnormal Productions, was one of those small but interesting Bukowski adaptations that quickly disappeared, rarely to be seen.

But Mrowca and his by-now group of hood/neighborhood toughs were not finished with the Bukowski oeuvre. The final edit was barely completed when the group embarked on a second short adaptation, *The Blanket*. "The Blanket," a Bukowski tale from the early 70's, is closer to traditional horror than *Lonely at the Top*. In it an only slight variation of a Bukowski anti hero struggles through surreal/hallucinatory stream of consciousness scenarios all centered around the notion of a blanket that may be trying to kill him. The story has the Chinaski-modeled character taking refuge with drunk neighbors on a lower floor with the blanket in hot pursuit. The story concludes when the protagonist, in a manic state,

99

picks up a knife and stabs the blanket before admitting to the reader that he must be truly mad.

The B-movie, and a bit schlocky attitude of *The Blanket* appealed to Mrowca, and the cast included John Hiler, Anthony Cannata and Debra Rodkin. Hiler, who has gone on to become a noted musical producer, mixer, arranger, composer and songwriter, recalled the experience.

Hiler was living in Chicago at the time, working on his own music and doing spot engineering jobs to pay the bills. He soon immersed himself in a thriving creative/bohemian community and crossed paths with aspiring filmmaker Gary Mrowca.

"Gary was a huge Bukowski fan," reflected Hiler. "I had not read Bukowski yet, but I was in the neighborhood. [I read] Miller, Burroughs, Ferlinghetti and other City Lights writers, but not Bukowski. Gary knew that there was an apartment above mine in the run-down building where I lived that was vacant, and he asked if I would be interested in playing Hank in a film adaptation of the Bukowski short story *The Blanket*. I was hesitant, not having acted since high school, but he explained that the movie would be mostly stop motion and voiceover. That was good enough for me. I was in."

There was just a small issue: how would somebody who didn't know Bukowski from Adam go about recreating one of the most well known literary mavericks on the planet? "To prepare, I hit the woodshed," reflected Hiler. "I researched Charles Bukowski. I read at least half a dozen of his books, and I watched hours of documentary footage that Barbet Schroeder filmed. I also relied heavily on Gary's excellent direction and his intimate knowledge of Hank and his world and where he came from. I was able to inhabit the role and, at least, play the imposter for a little while."

Along the way, Hiler's newfound respect for the mind of Bukowski as channeled into his participation in *The Blanket*. "I loved the idea that we were inhabiting a mind that was breaking down a grey space between reality and nightmare. To act as one who didn't know what was real and what was delirium, that was probably the biggest challenge for me."

The making of *The Blanket* was an exercise in surprising precision for Hiler. Navigating the world of stop motion literally in the dark and on film, the filmmakers did not know until the very end how the stop motion was meshing with actual film until filming was completed and the film was developed. Hiler saw the production as a well planned exercise, given the limitations of schedule, budget and the primitive nature of what Mrowca and company were attempting. "We were flying by the seat of our pants. We were shooting guerrilla style and rolling the dice in the hopes that it somehow came together in the end. And it did."

Although rarely seen, Hiler looks back fondly on what *The Blanket* accomplished. "The one great tragedy of this story is that Hank died before the film was completed, and Gary never got to show it to his idol."

Amor Por Menos (1994)

Bukowski's influence on the international stage of cinema could not be denied, especially when it came to Mexico. How Bukowski's style of writing translated in what has traditionally been a conservative religious and moral country is open to conjecture. But, as witness the 1994, 12 minute short film *Amor Por Menos*, some people were definitely getting Bukowski and his work.

The origin of *Amor Por Menos* is a bit sketchy but there is much that indicates that the Antonio Urrutia directed film may well have taken its cues from the psychologically dark and demented short story of mannequin love and obsession *Love for $17.50*, which first appeared in the Bukowski collection *South of No North* in 1973.

Amor Por Menos, which stars Carlos Aviles, Dominque Chapuy and Octavio Limon, is one of those maddeningly Bermuda Triangle Bukowski related obscurities. The only thing for certain is that it was made in 1994, reportedly received a scattering of screenings in Mexico and then promptly disappeared from the film consciousness. Director Urruttia would go on to a considerable career but, with the exception of occasional mentions in his filmography, press regarding the film was nonexistent.

For Bukowski film completists, *Amor Por Menos* is most certainly the missing link.

An Evil Town (1995)

Midway through the 90's, films adapted from Bukowski's stories were largely regulated to the shadows as far as the public was concerned.

Tales of Ordinary Madness and *Barfly,* thanks largely to their A-list casts and half hearted studio support, received the lions' share of notoriety from the critical press, but with the exception of some minor foreign press nods, were soon regulated to the status of oddities, and failed to lift Bukowski's public profile.

All of that changed in 1995 when fledgling director Richard Sears, attempting his first ever commercial film, turned the often staid Cannes Film Festival judges on their heads with a rough, raw and downright profane and depressing treatment of the dark/noir/psychological trials of a man in isolation and on dangerous psychological footing as he moves from town to town, a hair trigger away from doing great and violent things. This Charles Bukowski psychological terror tale originally appeared in the short story collection *Tales of Ordinary Madness* in 1972. *An Evil Town* became a 20-minute film masterwork, capturing top honors for best short film at the famed Cannes Film Festival with the award Le Semaine de la Critique and top honors from the prestigious New York Underground Film Festival.

Sears admitted that taking Bukowski to Cannes was nothing short of life changing. "I was just excited to be there. I couldn't believe we got into Cannes in the first place. I was totally shocked and surprised that we won at Cannes. That was an amazing out of body experience for me."

For Sears it would prove to be the culmination of a literary relationship with Bukowski that began during his time at San Francisco Art Institute. "I was a huge fan of Bukowski and still am. The first book I read was *Ham on Rye*, and I was hooked. I devoured everything else after that one. I enjoyed his brutal honesty, the way he romanticized the ugliness of life. He was able to bring you into his world and make you feel it."

An Evil Town, whose cast includes Keith Philips, Matt Cheese, John Johnson, Mike Kuchar, Greg Lucey and Nathaniel Roberts, is one of the more literal takes on a Bukowski work, magnifying the darkness and hopelessness of Frank Evans—a man lost in life and madness.

Sears, a dyed in the wool realist with a sense of irony and humor, had graduated from San Francisco Art Institute with a Fine Arts degree. But he knew that in the real world that degree and a dime… well, you get the picture. As he recalled in an interview with *The Los Angeles Times*, "I earned a degree, but there was not much help after graduation. There was no job placement. It was more like 'have a good life. Bye.'"

But Sears did have a lot going for him: an innate sense of story telling and style that appealed to an instinctive sense of fringe and unorthodox filmmaking. It also did not hurt that he was an avid Charles Bukowski reader and had developed a particular fondness for the story *An Evil Town*.

"I liked the build of the violence the story had," he explained to the author. "It kind of reminded me of *Taxi Driver*. When I read the story it reminded me of the Tenderloin area of San Francisco which is where I lived for a time as a student. I'd sometime see these old men in bars by themselves that seemed to be from a different era. I often wondered about their lives. Where did they work, live? They seemed to be lost and just wasting time doing nothing."

Spears, who recounted that he once ran into Bukowski at the race track but did not want to bother him, tracked down the rights for *An Evil Town* to City Lights Publishing, who were quick to agree to movie rights on any of the stories they had published in early Bukowski books. Shortly thereafter he made the acquaintance of a budding producer named Mat Lundberg who shared Spears' enthusiasm for the story. Now came the tough part: finding investors who would fund the project—to the tune of $30,000. The script that Sears and Lundberg presented to investors was a fairly straightforward eight to ten pages. But as the director recalled, it was a lot more complicated than that.

"Mat Lundberg and I scraped it together with all kinds of favors. It was challenging for people to read the script and understand my vision for the film. The pacing is methodical and slow, on purpose, in parts. But in the script people didn't see that. So I had to make people really understand what these scenes felt like before we made the film. That was a challenge to explain what was in my head to folks before we shot it."

What turned out to be in Sears' head during his maiden voyage into filmmaking was to be true to his source material. "I wanted to be 100 percent true to Bukowski's story and voice," he said. "I wanted to create this mysterious world/city that felt like a character in itself, like a city that was slowly destroying this man's mind. I wanted it to feel like *An Evil Town*." It was a feeling that continued once filming began on the miniscule three-day shoot in 1993.

Sears was on a mission to nail the story and mold it in Bukowski's image. "I added long, tracking, walking shots to express the loneliness one can feel in the city. I liked the idea that the main character, Frank Evans, was slowly going a bit insane from loneliness and isolation and then this strange man tries to break into his world and become intimate, which was the worst thing that could happen to him."

An Evil Town was ultimately completed in 1993. Sears remembered that bringing *An Evil Town* to the finish line was no easy task. "I think we did it in three days. I had to piece together shooting/shots due to our budget, so it may well have been five days. After shooting, we were all out of money and had to pull in favors for post production. I think it probably took us a year to finish the film."

Shortly thereafter, Sears and Lundberg managed to get a copy of the completed film to Bukowski, which to Sears' way of thinking would be the final validation of his work. "We did right by Bukowski and his work. 100 percent. I know he saw the film and the word we got back was that he liked it very much."

An Evil Town began to make the rounds of the festival circuit. "When we started to submit to the festivals, the process we slow and grinding. We were turned down by Sundance. Go figure."

An Evil Town would eventually find an audience. At the New York Underground Film Festival it came to the attention of festival head, director Todd Phillips. "Todd loved the film and he recommended we rush a print to screen for the Cannes committee. We quickly got a print over there and handed it over. It was scary because it was our only print."

Buoyed by the success at Cannes, *An Evil Town* became a mini "must see" on both sides of the Atlantic. "The film was much more popular in Europe than the US," Sears reflected. "It played all the big European festivals. And then the rest was history."

Horseshoe (1998)

If you are looking for a Bukowski-inspired film that has viewers choosing up sides, then the six minute short *Horseshoe*, based on a poem of the same name that appeared in the collection *Septuagenarian Stew*, will certainly peak your interest. Depending on who you talk to, *Horseshoe* is either a pretentious and not very well written film, or it is a very good film and a classic.

The concept of *Horseshoe*, directed by David Lodge and starring Alan Hickman, Lynn Waldegrave, Diane Simmons, voiceover actor Don Fellows and an actor who goes only by the first name of Louis, is minimalist to say the least. An elderly man is awakened from a sound sleep by a message reminding him of a dental appointment he has that day. The man walks serenely through blocks of tall buildings to the dentist's office where the dentist makes a mold of his teeth (the mold being the horseshoe shaped appliance of the title). The dentist is not happy with the mold and another mold is taken. A voiceover narration of the Bukowski poem plays out over this lack of action. End of story and film.

On the surface, *Horseshoe* is, literally, not much, even by artsy, self-indulgent standards. But through the dearth of inaction and mundane moments there are some cinematic moments of moderate interest. Lodge chose to invest the film with a retro style scratchy film look and occasional moments of sepia tone. Fellows' serviceable rendition of the Bukowski poem is a nice counter to the hypnotic and soothing feel of the film that, at its most generous, is an acknowledgement of the mundane nature of old age.

A film so un-Bukowski-like and trivial would have seemed destined for immediate obscurity, but *Horseshoe* did manage a blip on the cultural scene when it captured The Juror's Prize for Best Short Film at the 1998 Cannes Film Festival. You can catch this film on one of several available internet platforms. Take a look and judge for yourself.

Clive Saunders' Excellent Bukowski Adventure

Filmmaker Clive Saunders is the prototypical working class Brit: cocksure, persistent, a bit of a hustler, with a blue collar, fuck you attitude. He was seemingly the ideal type to go all rough and tumble in the name of Bukowski. That he would attempt to make sense of the Bukowski tale *Love for $17.50*, an extreme bit of business that, among other niceties, shows the lead character having brutal and quite graphic sex with a mannequin, seems to make perfect sense. How he got to make that film is a story as good as Bukowski's tale.

"I was an actor in London in the early 90's," Saunders recalled during a US to UK hookup. "I was going to auditions and getting little shitty parts. Finally I said fuck this and went to the States. I got a job in real estate and then one day I was given a check for five grand to go and become an actor. So there I was in Los Angeles, living in a little apartment. My nextdoor neighbor was a big fat guy who got all these parts in Sylvester Stallone films. I was drinking with him one day and the subject of Bukowski came up. I didn't know who Bukowski was. I said 'Who's Bukowski?' He pulled out an old ratty copy of South Of No North and said, "Read this." I read it and it blew my fucking mind. This was the best shit I had ever read." A year later, Saunders' career was going nowhere. "I was out of work. What the fuck was I supposed to do?"

Enter Bukowski. Saunders kept returning to the work of Bukowski and, in particular, to the stories *Love for $17.50*, *The Devil Was Hot* and *Loneliness*. Saunders was ultimately inspired to the point where he decided that he would somehow obtain the rights to those stories, and do something—a screenplay, a theater production. Saunders was not sure, but he was quick to put his plan in action and to go to the source.

"I wrote to John Martin (Black Sparrow Books) to try and get the film rights. I also wrote to Bukowski. I told him I wasn't interested in his stories for commercial purposes, I wasn't going to add any shit to his stories and that I just wanted to adapt his stories theatrically. As it turned out, Bukowski was very ill at the time and in the hospital. But I did hear back from his agent who said Bukowski wanted $500 for the rights to those stories. So I sent him a check for $500 and got the okay."

Now that the rights were his, Saunders thought long and hard about what he wanted to do with them. "Making a film had not crossed my mind at that point. But I saw doing something with those Bukowski stories was the way out that I was looking for. So I contacted some actors and poets I knew back in London and said, 'If I can raise some money, let's put this out as a fringe theater piece and have some fun.'"

It was 1993, and Saunder's Bukowski theatrical experience which included *Love for $17.50* had its shakedown cruise way Off-Off Broadway in England at a fringe theater. Saunders recalled that those early performances were not very well attended, but that the production inspired a definite "lets put on a show" spirit that saw Saunders, the actor, playing the pivotal mannequin sex character in the *Love for $17.50* segment. "The mannequin scene was a real method scene," laughed Saunders. "So I really had to fuck it. But I had to be careful because I didn't want to cum on the first row."

Word of mouth ensued, and the Bukowski play began to do very well. "Eventually the play moved to a different theater and it started getting a little buzz," remembered Saunders. "It wasn't so much that a grown man was fucking a mannequin, but that this guy was doing Bukowski. Around that time I got a call from this theater guy in Los Angeles who wanted me to come back to LA to play a role in his play. So I go back to Los Angeles and I'm working with this theater group and I think that maybe my career is finally going to happen and maybe I can get in on the freak ticket. So I wrote a screenplay based on the Bukowski short stories. I wanted to make a film, but I knew nothing about filmmaking."

"So I'm talking to people. I wanted to make a feature. So I decided to track Linda Bukowski down. I contacted Linda and faxed over some reviews of the London shows. I was acting in another play at the time and I invited her to come down and see it. So the night of the play Linda arrives in a limo, the door opens and a whole lot of her gang are falling out drunk. It was like the circus had arrived. They saw the play and the next thing I know is I'm in the limo with Linda and all these drunk people and going somewhere with them."

Saunders related that Linda and he hit it off immediately. "Hank had only been dead a year or two. So she was still grieving heavily and so she was drinking. But she was quite a smart woman. She said 'Before I give you the rights, I want you to reproduce the play you did in London.' So I put it on in a place called Al's Bar for four nights. The guy handling the lights was a junkie and he kept missing his cues. It just didn't seem to be coming together. Fortunately the night Linda came to see it, it did come together."

Then came the double cross.

"Linda said 'I won't give you the rights to do the whole film. Now you've got to do a short film of 'Love for $17.50' before I give you the rights to do the whole film.'"

"And I said what the fuck! I had nothing better to do, so I said alright."

Love for $17.50 (1998)

Bukowski's stories were truly well-traveled when it came to the international filmmaking community. No story is more evident of this than *Love For $17.50*. Be it the compact nature of the tale or the intimate and raw characterization amid its fantastic trappings, filmmakers keep coming back to the basic tale in a variety of ways. *Amor Mon Mentos* was a Mexican take in 1994, while the 2002 over-the-top absurdist, lighthearted and farcical take spun the tale in a seemingly unusual PG-13 style. Sandwiched in between those was *Love for $17.50*, done up with a very British approach by director Clive Saunders in his subtle yet straightforward 25-minute short in 1998.

Saunders' take on the Bukowski story, which features Mickey Swenson and Tom Waldman, is a fairly straightforward affair. A lonely man's infatuation with a thrift store mannequin and the inevitable fall into insanity and dark fantasy are true to Bukowski's oeuvre of obsession as a springboard to all kinds of weirdness. It's out there if a bit harder to find than many Bukowski-related films, but those who have seen it give it an A for effort.

Also an A for sheer audacity and attitude. Saunders admitted to being less than thrilled, initially, about just doing *Love for $17.50*. "I wanted to do *The Devil Was Hot*. It was weird. It was hot. But nobody else wanted to do it."

The dust had hardly settled on the deal for *Love for $17.50* when it finally dawned on Saunders that he was in over his head. "It was my first time directing and I didn't know how to direct traffic." Saunders managed a solid backing team with producer Susan Rodgers and cinematographer Luc Niknair. "I was a purist about this story. I did not feel the need to do anything to this stuff. My attitude was that if I can spit this fucker out of my craw, then I could get on with my career."

For cinematographer Luc Niknair, *Love for $17.50* would also prove an opportunity to conquer new creative lands. "I was contacted by the producer who knew about my cinematography background," Niknair said. "And she also knew that I was willing to work for nothing. I was very good at videos, but I needed to shoot a narrative project. Clive [Saunders] had written the script and it looked like he was going to direct. The producer asked me what I thought of Clive directing this, and I said 'absolutely.'"

Niknair knew what he was in for. *Love for $17.50* was nothing if not controversial. "I was not afraid of controversial. What I knew was that Clive, coming from a theater background and this being his first film, was going to have to rely on me to help him execute the film visually and to help him tell the story."

The cinematographer's knowledge of Bukowski was limited to the movie *Barfly*. But during a crash course in all things Bukowski he would discover what he perceived as the way to go with the film. "I learned that Bukowski secretly loved film noir movies. For me that would be the cue, the hook. I knew it was an adult, gritty world that we were going to walk into. The story is about this character being in control of his love life. Until the point where he starts losing it."

With producer Rogers ramrodding the production, Saunders went ahead with getting financing for the film. "We had to go cap in hand to get the budget. Initially we figured $25-$35,000 would be enough."

Filming for *Love for $17.50* began in 1998 with a projected eight to 10 day shoot in Los Angeles. But before the first bit of film was shot, Saunders recalled that there were still quite a few hoops for him to jump through. "We found a thrift store location that we didn't have to buy. We called in a lot of favors. We went to a mannequin factory and told them we needed a mannequin for a short film and we got it for free. We didn't tell them that we were going to fuck it and beat it up. We did request an extra large mannequin with a big ass because these had to be Bukowski kind of women."

By the time filming began on *Love for $17.50*, an estimated 8-10 day shoot of Los Angeles exteriors and soundstage sets, Niknair has already developed a shorthand for making the film, especially on the interiors. "I was prepared to always watch the choreography of what the director was doing. It was basically done at a down and dirty clip between me and Clive. We chose to go hand held [camera] to create a dark and hard energy. The scene in the kitchen where he tries to rape the mannequin, I just went on instinct when we shot that. When the mannequin gets destroyed by the girlfriend, we really didn't know how that was going to happen. We just went for it."

Things appeared to be going smoothly leading up to the start of filming until it came time for casting the title character, the psychotic mannequin-fucker. At that point, Saunders recalled, he was getting a lot of input and no small amount of pressure. "There was a lot of pressure on me to play the character because I had played him in the theater productions, but I was going to have enough going on in making the film so I refused. I had found this actor named Mickey Swenson, an older guy who was perfect for the part. But then my producer Susan calls and says the actor Adam Goldberg wants to play the guy. Now at the time Adam Goldberg was this hot new actor on the scene. No disrespect to Adam Goldberg but if an actor in his 20's does what goes on in this film, the whole thing suddenly becomes *American Pie*. If a guy in his 50's does what he does in this film, it's like, 'Shit, he's not coming back from that.' During the audition we even had Tom Hanks' brother, Jim Hanks turn up. Linda Bukowski was also around during the casting and she had some input."

Saunders ended up getting his way when it came to getting Mickey Swenson, but would ultimately be disappointed when the actress he championed for the pivotal girlfriend-flips-out scene was overruled in favor of another actress, effectively winning the war but losing a battle.

"In those days, you had to build a crummy apartment set on a soundstage and that ended up taking a big bite out of the budget. Filming itself was a joy, but by the time we had finished filming we had run out of money, and had no money for editing and post-production. I had quite simply run out of money."

Saunders was in the dumps on the day he was invited to a superbowl party and made the acquaintance of a Japanese guy and struck up a conversation. "Neither of us were into American football, and so we got to talking. I told him 'I'm stuck. I shot this film, I'm living in a crappy motel, I ran out of dough and couldn't afford the editing suites to cut the film.' He asked me how much it would cost to finish the film? I told him about $15,0000-$20,000. He pulled out his checkbook and wrote me a check for $20,000."

In short order, Saunders had edited a final cut for *Love for $17.50*. He recalled what happened next. "I figured it (the film) would have a minor little roll out. It was never a commercial film, and nobody was going to put it on television. I did it to get to make the Bukowski feature. I wanted to make a fucking film that would be good enough for Linda [Bukowski] so that I could make the feature."

"But all of a sudden it became huge. We did a screening at the Vogue Theater in Hollywood, put the title 'Bukowski Movie' on the marquee, brought in some cheap alcohol and put the word out. It was crazy sold out. It was a great night."

Niknair looks back fondly on the film. "It was my first narrative film. At the time I was like 'Man! I could have done this better.' But it still holds its own. I'm in awe of how ballsy it was in what we did. Those scenes with the mannequin, people would be flipping out if they saw this now. With the way things are now we would have a tough time making this film today. But at the end of the day, this is really an anti-man story."

The saga of *Love for $17.50* would have a bittersweet ending. Following the unexpected buzz from *Love For $17.50*, Saunders was offered his first full length feature directing job in the true crime drama *Gacy*, based, loosely, on the grizzly true life exploits of serial killer John Wayne Gacy. Saunders, ever the realist, took the gig with misgivings, as at the time it was the only game in town. *Gacy*, amid a rush of bad reviews, would barely make it to video, and, as Saunders expected, word got back to Linda Bukowski who, coincidentally, rescinded the feature film rights for the Bukowski material. Saunders, who to this day continues to pop up in small, obscure projects, looks back on his *Love for $17.50* experience with a literal shrug of the shoulders.

"I gave it my best. It didn't achieve what I set out for it to do. I made the short so I could make the feature and stay in Hollywood. Things just didn't turn out that way."

Going into 2000

By the 2000s, filmmakers had definitely given the Bukowski film challenge the old college try. There have been interesting documentaries, a handful of relatively ambitious features that were occasionally very good and have won a number of awards, but never were there what one could call breakout commercial hits. There were a number of shorts, student films, and art house efforts, and brave and often good surreal stylistic experiments.

But by then, Bukowski on film still seemed a niche category. There were devotees salivating and speculating on the internet and in website chats while most of the rest of the civilized world was continuing to ask, 'Bukowski who?' Where Bukowski's movie adventures seemed to be going was anybody's guess.

Black Sparrow publisher John Martin put it succinctly and mildly hopefully in a 2000 interview with the lit magazine *Free Thought* when he said, "I could care less about the films, unless, by some chance, someday, a really good screenwriter and director get involved."

The Man with the Beautiful Eyes (2000)

The film *The Man with the Beautiful Eyes* is as complex as it is brief. Clocking in at a mere five minutes and faithfully adapted from the poem of the same name that appeared in Bukowski's last collection of poetry before his death, 1992's *The Last Night of the Earth Poems*, the film is alternately weird, creepy and psychologically telling of the duplicity implicit in Bukowski's world view.

Directed by animation auteur Jonathan Hodgson in conjunction with illustrator Jonny Hannah, the film is an examination of two worlds colliding: that of daring childhood and an adult world rife with responsibility and prejudice. It was an unorthodox but no less valid examination of what lies between the lines in Bukowski's stories.

The Man with the Beautiful Eyes is a dark and striking tale of a gang of children who, against the express warnings of their parents, wander around an unkempt house and come face to face with its resident, a very Chinaski-like caricature, swilling beer in the middle of the day, looking the very opposite of their parents. The children immediately see this man as a symbol of independent freedom, the very thing their parents have warned them about. The film plays out with the man's house mysteriously burning to the ground. The children believe that their parents have done it.

This brief exercise is highly ambitious. Illustrated as a mixture of paint, ink and collage, *The Man with the Beautiful Eyes* is the conceit of outsider art as art which is Hodgson's stock in trade. Hodgson admits to being a meticulous and somewhat naïve filmmaker who is at his best, he thinks, when dealing with a short form project. "I prefer working with the short animation format which allows me more freedom of expression. When making a short film you can usually be looser and more experimental with technique and narrative."

The very out-of-kilter animation sense of *The Man with the Beautiful Eyes* is both subtle and in one's face, and was the first of several animated short films of Bukowski's work.

Bring Me Your Love (2000)

This first legitimate adaptation of the Bukowski short story *Bring Me Your Love*—second adaptation for completists if you count the initial bargain basement student film in which the director refused to give his real name years earlier—carries with it a much glossier pedigree. Director David Morrissey, a much more mature filmmaker, was pretty much quick and to the point when he told *Netribution.co.uk* about his approach to making cinematic sense of the 1983 Bukowski/R. Crumb collaboration. "I read the short story. I loved it. I really thought that it would make a good adaptation, then just got it together and did it. Really, that was it."

It is safe to say that Morrissey did a right representative and literal take on the Bukowski story: Journalist visits his wife in an asylum where she berates him, accusing him of cheating on her with another woman. He denies the infidelity and is soon off to a nearby hotel and a rendezvous with another woman. The tryst is unexpectedly interrupted by a phone call from his wife who continues to accuse him, as the other woman smirks in the background. The wife hangs up, the man and woman continue to fight. The phone rings again and the insanity continues as they both grab for it.

The cast: Ian Hart, Simon Lenagan, Barbara Hartwell and Saira Todd, turn in solid portrayals, one that had the reviewer in *The Independent* praising the film as "a bitter duet between love and betrayal." This 16-minute effort had limited art house and festival exposure before going the way of many Bukowski efforts—gone but primed for reexamination.

Broken Mirror Music (2001)

Director Andre Alfa is well aware that his Bukowski-inspired movie *Broken Mirror Music* is hard to find, and that one just has to know where to look. In a recent conversation, Alfa was quick to shorten the search. "The only place it was ever screened was at the Los Angeles Film School. I did give a few DVD copies to friends and family. But these days the only place to see it now is on Vimeo."

Alfa, a no-frills filmmaker who, after years of making shorts, commercials and music videos recently completed his first feature film (the horror thriller *Blackstock Boneyard*), is a prototypical Bukowski adherent to all things Bukowski, heavy on the enthusiasm and admiration. "I've been a longtime fan of Bukowski. I have always been drawn to his raw honesty, his dark humor and how he went about portraying the underbelly of Los Angeles."

Broken Mirror Music, whose cast includes Ken Beider, Kristen Loris, Nina Shay, Mark Lambert and Susanna Midnight, is a taut examination and dichotomy of a whole lot of Bukowski trademarks: the loneliness, the frustration and the constant attempts and constant failures wrapped in irony that are Bukowski touchstones. A lonely and disillusioned Bukowski type, big on booze, classical music and low class and equally lonely women, pines for something better in life and, in desperation, posts a "Woman Wanted" flyer on a car in the aftermath of his latest flame throwing him over for a stranger in a bar. A woman replies to the flyer and comes to his apartment where she is treated to an uneasy yet eloquent soliloquy about the balance between sex, love and relationships. The woman freaks out when our hero comes on a little too strong and rushes from the room just as his old flame turns up, tearful, in the aftermath of her ill-fated bar hookup. He slaps her across the face and then lets her in, realizing that his dreams are also ill-fated, and that this is as good as it gets.

For a film that almost nobody has seen, *Broken Mirror Music* is a powerful interpretation of Bukowski and his work. Alfa offered that the film was an amalgamation of three Bukowski works, the poem "Fire Station" from the collection *Play the Piano Drunk Like a Percussion Instrument Until the Fingers Begin to Bleed a Bit*, the poem "The Soldier, His Wife and the Bum*"* from the book *The Last Night of the Earth Poems* and the short story *Loneliness* from the collection *South of No North*.

Alfa recalled that the film was conceived during his time as a student at the Los Angeles Film School. As a student film, Alfa apparently had no prospects for making money off the film, but he made a point of getting permission to use the source material. "I'm not sure the Bukowski estate ever knew about this film. I did go to Bukowski's publisher, John Martin, and, since it was a student film with no intention of trying to generate income from it, he gave me the go ahead."

Getting funding for the film was a whole other matter. Alfa hinted at the fact that Bukowski's approach to some of the seedier sides of life had been a turnoff to potential investors. "I finally ended up funding it myself out of pocket (an estimated $3,000). The budget was stretched to the limit during a rather ambitious, compressed schedule that included several Los Angeles locations.

"The film definitely had its challenges," acknowledged Alfa, "mainly due to the shoestring budget and shooting everything on location. But staying true to Bukowski's work was the biggest challenge."

And as the few who have seen *Broken Mirror Music* will attest to, Alfa's little-seen interpretation gets high marks. "I would like to think Bukowski would have liked it. I tried to get it right, and, to my way of thinking, it was not misdone."

Apporte-Moi Ton Amour (2002)

There is not a lot to say about this French entry, an 11-minute umpteenth remake of the Bukowski warhorse *Give Me Your Love*.

It was directed by controversial former soccer player Eric Cantona who, at the time, was just beginning a second career as an actor, and his first-ever directing attempt with *Apporte-Moi Ton Amour*. Shot in France, with a cast that toplined Lawa Loire, Daniel Duval, Nadia Fares and Jacques Hansen, the film, by all accounts, is a fairly literal translation of the Bukowski story. It is an exercise in insanity and infidelity, and the consequences of both. Despite having made the film, director Cantana had little to say about it.

In a translation from the *Bukowski Forum* of a conversation with a French television interviewer, we get this much from Cantana. "The story is about paranoia, blah blah blah, paranoia, blah blah blah, paranoia." Apparently, *Apporte-Moi Ton Amour* made a little bit of critical noise, capturing an award in 2003 at the International Festival Of Film And Television Cinema. That is all.

Son of Satan (2003)

Bukowski's life is on display in just about everything Bukowski has written, One does not have to look very deeply to discover what the author had to say to the world in his short story *Son of Satan*.

"I had some pretty terrible parents," Bukowski was quoted, in the book *Bukowski for Beginners* by Carlos Polimeni. "And your parents are pretty much your whole world. That's all there is."

Consequently, if Bukowski had ever decided to sit down and write a formal memoir, the chances are real good that *Son of Satan* would have made a dandy introduction to his world. Written when the author was in his 70's in 1987, and published in the collection *Septuagenarian Stew* in 1990, *Son of Satan* is raw, primal and downright profane on so many levels. In a poverty-stricken neighborhood, the 11 year-old leader of a gang of boys turns his anger and boredom on a neighborhood kid who had, allegedly, been bragging about a sexual encounter that nobody believed actually happened. The gang corners the boy, beats him up and then hangs him. The boy survives the hanging, tells his parents who, in turn, tell the boy's father who confronts his son and proceeds to beat the crap out of him. The story concludes with the boy cowering under his bed and vowing to one day kill his father. The end.

Son of Satan is easily one of Bukowski's more visceral, in your face stories, the subtle-as-trainwreck message being how violence, in all its base and raw moments, can be passed down the generations; in this case from father to son. Film director J.J. Villard, who has gone on to become a leading light in animation, put it this way in conversation with *Kill Pretty Magazine*. "It really was a dark film."

In taking *Son of Satan* to the screen, which featured the stark voiceover work of Tony Ortiz and John Savenzer, Villard employed roughly-sketched pencil and crayon drawings that captured the requisite savagery of the tale. The film was conceived as a very early student project while Villard was a student at the California Institute of the Arts, and was very much a DIY project cut together on a limited time and budget.

Most student films of the time had a lifespan of one or two showings before disappearing into a musty box never to be seen again. But that would not be the case with *Son of Satan*. Villard was very much a hustler at that point, and rather than let it disappear, he took it upon himself to get the film out there to the masses.

"I managed to get the film to Linda Bukowski," Villard told *Kill Pretty Magazine*. "She saw it, loved it and gave me the rights to put the film in festivals. I am in debt to her forever."

Villard, on his own dime, took *Son of Satan* on a barnstorming tour of several international film festivals before landing at Cannes, where it managed to capture the prize for best short film. The irony of what happened was not lost on Villard. "Cannes is where word got around, and DreamWorks heard about me and offered me a job. The first thing I did for DreamWorks was *Shrek 3*. It's all kind of nuts, because *Son of Satan* was really a dark and dirty film."

But perhaps the highest compliment to *Son of Satan's* place in the Bukowski cinematic world has to go to *Ottawa Animation Festival Director* Chris Robinson. "It's a ball breaking Bukowski short," he enthused. "*Son of Satan* is raw, nasty, violent and disturbing."

Bukowski: Born into This (2003)

By all accounts, the late documentary filmmaker John Dullaghan was a man obsessed with Charles Bukowski. What many critics consider a definitive magnum opus, the two hour and ten minute documentary *Bukowski: Born into This*, was created by Dullaghan, who spent 15 years looking for Bukowski: where he lived, traveled, how he grew up, how he lived his life and tracking down the people both close and distant, famous and obscure who were willing to sit for an interview and tell the filmmaker what they knew about the "real" Bukowski.

For Dullaghan, the come-to-Jesus moment that led to *Bukowski: Born into This* was deeply personal, as he related in an interview with the literary magazine *Free Thought* in 2000. "This has become very much a life's work. Bukowski's writing just had a real profound effect on me. I was at a point in my life where a lot of us wind up, a point where you're in a job or a career that is just killing you. After reading *Post Office*, I saw the things that he went through and they weren't just the things that he went through, but in my office and every office. I was in the corporate world and wound up in the hospital due to the stress that I was going through working 60 hour weeks. When I read Bukowski it really made me reassess things."

Dullaghan's odyssey to *Bukowski: Born into This* (whose working title was *Walk Through the Fire: The Life of Charles Bukowski*) was rife with challenges. He was learning the filmmaking process on the fly without any experience or education. The nuts and bolts of the filmmaking process were well beyond his pay grade, but he knew how to approach people who knew Bukowski at various points in his life and career, and how to get them to talk about him. At the end of the day, Dullaghan had something that cut through most of those pitfalls associated with making such a film.

"I was passionate about what I was doing," he told *Indiwire.com*. "I was serious about it. I wanted to do the best job that I could."

In Dullaghan's mind that meant *Bukowski: Born into This* would be non-narrative in nature, relying to a large extent on old archival interview and performance footage of Bukowski. But Dullaghan proved fearless in approaching Sean Penn, U2's Bono, actor Harry Dean Stanton, singer/songwriter Tom Waits, *Black Sparrow* publisher John Martin and a wide array of old drinking buddies, fellow workers from his post office days, fellow writers, and, a testament to his persistence: Linda Bukowski and Bukowski's daughter Marina.

"When I came to this project all I knew was the Bukowski myth," Dullaghan recalled in conversations with *Film Threat* and *Indiwire.com*. "I created the film not just for the Bukowski fanatics. They're going to like whatever you put out there. I tried to make this accessible to people who may have just heard the name Bukowski for the first time. If Bukowski was just about sex and violence, you could get that anywhere. But it's that other thing: it's what he brings to his work as a human being; that's what makes him special. To hear stories about him crying when he saw *Star Wars*, that's not what we think of Bukowski. That's what I was after."

Dullaghan went on to say that people were really cooperative when he approached them, sensing his sincerity about Bukowski. Insights were around every corner, such as when he approached fellow workers from Bukowski's years at the post office for their memories.

"I talked to a few people. and the impression that I got was that he was quiet, kept to himself, but that he really knew his stuff. If someone had a question about an address or zip code, they would ask Bukowski and he would know immediately."

In the *Free Thought* interview Dullaghan explained that he had equally good luck with the notoriously reclusive actor Sean Penn, whose tales of his encounters with Bukowski, personally and professionally around the time of *Barfly*, had long been oft-repeated. "I have to say that interviewing Sean Penn was probably the most memorable interview because you don't get to talk to Sean Penn everyday."

The filmmaker supplemented interviews with hours of researching the Bukowski archives, thus an immense output of Bukowski material became evident. "Most writers are lucky to get out a few good chapbooks in their lifetime. Bukowski turned out thousands of poems," he said.

But making *Bukowski: Born into This* did result in Dullaghan facing some uncomfortable, albeit amusing moments, as he recounted in

Indiwire.com. "I had gone to Germany to film, and I guess Bukowski had gone there in 1978 and had torn up this hotel. When I got to the hotel and told them who I was and what I was doing they started yelling at me and told me to get off their property."

Dullaghan did not have to go abroad to discover that Bukowski's reputation had preceded him. "At one point, I went to Bukowski's childhood home on Longwood Avenue. It was in a pretty bad part of town, and it really looked like a crack house. While we were there, this old guy who lived there came by and started screaming at us and kicked us off the property, yelling 'You goddamned Bukowski people!' I guess he had had it up to his eyeballs with Bukowski showing up and tramping all over his property. I totally understood where he was coming from and we left."

By the year 2000 Dullaghan had more than 200 hours of footage, and would spend the next four years hustling to get more money to edit the film and deal with distribution. "Right now, the vast majority of the filming is done," he reported to *Free Thought*, "and I'm at the point where I'm getting further funding to finish it. So it's going to take some time, but the end is definitely in sight."

Bukowski: Born into This, clocking in at a robust two hours 10 minutes, had what amounted to its first public screening on January 18, 2003 at the prestigious and hip Sundance Film Festival, followed in October 9, 2003 at the Austin Film Festival. Not surprisingly, there was a lot of critical and public interest in Dullaghan's documentary, in 2004 and into 2005 in Europe and Asia screenings were to sold out audiences in the United Kingdom, Sweden, France, Denmark, Finland, Poland, Japan and, almost a given, in Germany. To critic and "real person" alike, *Bukowski: Born into This* was praised as the definitive look at Bukowski at both his best and his worst.

Words like "powerful," "raw," "profane," "human," "engaging" and "fascinating" were some of the compliments Dullaghan and his film received. Dullighan remained humble and grateful in the wake of the praise for his maiden effort, and equally appreciative of Bukowski—the man who inspired him.

"One of the things that I really hope for is that my film counteracts that image of the drunken lowlife who also happened to write. He was one of the great literary artists of our time."

There's a Bukowski poem called "Roll The Dice" and it starts:

If you're going to try
Go all the way
This could mean losing girlfriends
Wives
Relatives
Jobs
And maybe your mind
It's a test of your endurance
Of how much you really want to do it

Dullaghan took Bukowski's poem to heart. *Bukowski: Born into This* is how much he really wanted to do it.

My Old Man (2004)

Bukowski's relationship with his father is well known. And to hear the author talk about it in interviews and through a large percentage of his creative output, it was not a good one. Physically and emotionally abusive to the nth degree, his father's cruelty seems fairly obvious. Bukowski, as quoted in an *American Futures* website article, was beaten three times a week by his father from the ages of six to eleven. But in his own ravaged life and attitude, he saw those beatings as a major influence on his life and attitude. "When you get the shit kicked out of you long enough, you learn to say exactly what you mean. You get all the pretension kicked out of you."

That was exactly what fledgling filmmaker Alex Levine had in mind when he tackled a seven-minute interpretation of the Bukowski poem "My Old Man" in 2004. Levine, who has gone on to have a long and prosperous career in Canada's science fiction television industry, took Bukowski at his word. The poem begins with a young Hank drunk and in emotional distress, finding his father having tossed his short stories in the garbage. In the end he has a relationship moment when his father finds a story that he really likes.

The film, whose cast includes Glynis Davies, Tom McBeath and Brent Stait, is a slight but effective interpretation, true to Bukowski's world, and, within the confines of a spartan production on a shoestring $20,000 budget, shows just the right amount of reverence for Bukowski and managing to maintain the author's true intent.

My Old Man had an official unveiling in August 2004. It sank into the mists too quickly to avoid popular inspection, and is well worth tracking down. Happy hunting.

Factotum (2005)

Poke any Bukowski movie observer long enough and eventually the subject of *Factotum* comes up. To a person, they swear by the fact that the 2005 film version, directed by Bent Hamer and starring Matt Dillon as the titular Henry Chinaski, may well be the best Bukowski adaptation of all time.

Factotum is a hybrid on several levels. It is a French/Norwegian co production based on the Bukowski book *Factotum*, as well as bits and pieces of the Bukowski collections *The Days Run Away Like Horses Over the Hills*, *What Matters Most is How You Walk Through the Fire* and *The Captain is Out to Lunch and the Sailors Have Taken Over the Ship*. Despite *Factotum* being firmly entrenched in 1940's Los Angeles mythology, the film carries with it a very "now" vibe and was filmed in Minneapolis. At its core, *Factotum* comes across as an artistic piece of dirty cinema realism that is both reverent and has a sense of raw reality that is conspicuous in it's adherence to Bukowski's dark days.

The film follows Henry Chinaski through his endless series of short-lived dead end jobs, his endless drunken hours in seedy dive bars and the equally low life women who drift in and out of his life. At the crossroads of a down and out life, Chinaski persists in his attempts—real or imagined—to become a writer. *Factotum* in the director's hands is Hollywood, but, at the same time, not Hollywood. The expected twists and turns of the big studio epics are not there. The surprises are not surprises but rather a straight, no frills look at Bukowski at his most direct and in your face. *Factotum* is Chinaski a/k/a Bukowski, which, according to director Hamer, was the biggest challenge.

"Factotum offered little in the way of a dramatic arc," Hamer reflected in a *Today.com* interview, "because the reality of Bukowski/Chinaski is that he refuses to change. He has his own view and he's presenting it generously, but don't come to try and change that view.

I didn't try to capture the book literally on film, but rather to present an interpretation of the man and his work."

Hamer was no novice coming to *Factotum*. He had earned his stripes in Europe and had a breakout hit overseas with the film *Kitchen Stories*. He would come to *Factotum* loaded for bear with a script co-written with Jim Jarmusch and veteran screenwriter Jim Stark who also signed on as producer. But while it was being trumpeted as a US/Norwegian production, Hamer had to deal with US filmmaking rules and regulations often on the fly. Still, he remained confident as he recalled in a *Cineuropa* conversation. "*Factotum* is a low budget film like those I usually make back home. The difference with this film is that I had the chance to work with big stars, and they were interested in working with me. In a sense, it wasn't even a real Hollywood situation."

Since Bukowski's passing his ex wife Linda Bukowski had become both the gatekeeper and final word on anybody attempting to make a cinematic run at Bukowski. She had been witness to myriad attempts to capture the essence of Bukowski, and in hindsight and with no small amount of frustration had watched as portrayals of the author and his alter ego Henry Chinaski that missed the mark. But she was hopeful that Hamer's version of Factotum would get it right, as she explained on *Today.com*.

"He [Bukowski] means to speak to everybody but everybody isn't ready. We're afraid to look at our own warts and moles and wrinkles and all of that."

And so, with expectations, good and bad, already hanging over the project, the pressure to cast a powerful and perfect Chinaski was at its peak when Hamer announced that actor Matt Dillon would play the ultimate Bukowski alter ego. Dillon, already in his 40's by this time, had built quite the rep as a pretty boy teen star/ by the numbers action hero/he-man, and had survived Hollywood typecasting by turning his talents, in later years, to darker and edgier adult films such as *Crash*.

At first Dillon seemed a solid choice to play Chinaski. He was a capable actor, adaptable to whatever challenges a role might require. But even with an initial endorsement from Hamer, their early meetings were colored by indecision. The director conceded that he was not convinced that Dillon could physically manifest the right image for Chinaski. The actor remembered sharing Hamer's doubts, in conversation with *Movielab.com*. "I was like 'Are you sure you got the right guy?' Once he made it clear that I wasn't expected to play Charles [Bukowski]. but rather his alter ego named Hank, it gave me a sense of relief."

But Dillon now had the sense of physicality branded in his psyche. To help ease his way into the character of both Chinaski and Bukowski, the actor turned to somebody who might have the best insights, Bukowski's wife Linda. "I talked to his wife Linda," he related to *Movielab.com*. "She said he [Bukowski] always felt misunderstood, and that it really bothered him when he was depicted as dirty, unwashed and a kind of a slob. She told me that the reality was that he was always very neat."

But that did not stop the actor, per the requirements of *Factotum*, from morphing into the image of a down and out loser. "I grew a beard and my hair was done a certain way," he told *Movielab.com*. "I put on a little weight. I let myself go. Hank was a guy who was physically defeated. The way he carried himself physically was that the material world sort of defeated him."

Dillon jumped into the opportunity that *Factotum* offered with a sense of method, and he approached Bukowski's ragged life as a mirror on every man who hates his job and his life and is essentially going through the motions. He prepped for the role by becoming a student of Bukowski, reading his work and watching endless hours of interviews. Dillion, in conversation with *IGN.com*, particularly relished dealing with Chinaski's legendary drinking habits. "It may sound simple enough to play a drunk, but there's actually a lot of different ways to go. Hank [Bukowski] is a marathon drinker. He's a professional. He's an unapologetic drunk."

The *Factotum* production made extensive use of the Minneapolis bar district, with many of the pivotal scenes unfolding in such local watering holes as *The Depot Bar*, *The Dubliner* and *Cuzzy's*. Although everybody was taking this project seriously, Dillon carried the heaviest load: his character addressed a multitude of challenges that included excessive drinking, the aversion to holding even the simplest of jobs, and tenuous relationships with women. The actor did this while staying focused on getting it right by Bukowski, and, by association, doing Henry Chinaski justice.

"Some movies you've got to stay focused and stay in character more throughout the day, otherwise you lose it," he explained to *Entertainment Weekly*. "In that sense I had to keep Hank close. If I moved away from him for too long then I'd have to ramp up again. At the end of the day I was able to leave the character behind me. But I would go home and spend the time away from the set reading Bukowski or watching interviews he did. That was the kind of thing that kept me focused."

Hamer put Dillon through the paces of Chinaski's seemingly never-ending and, yes, often funny attempts at employment at its most brutal and demeaning, and, in the process, the actor found himself respecting Chinaski and his struggles.

"His [Bukowski's] is a working class hero," the actor told *Fox News*. "Ninety eight percent of people are not living their dreams on the job. These are the people that are fueling Bukowski's writing. He's right in the thick of it."

Factotum had its official release in Europe in 2005, where it would go on to garner respectable box office and eventually a handful of critical awards, before having its limited United States/North American release in 2006. Not surprisingly, Bukowski's world as explored in *Factotum* was greeted with mixed results. After two promising weeks, the arrival of Labor Day saw *Factotum* sink into relative obscurity in record time. *Factotum's* reported $1 million budget would bring in a bit more than $3,000,000 total, and yet another Bukowski film adaptation that would fail, commercially, to capture the public's imagination. Nevertheless, director Hamer, in conversation with *Today.com*, was quite pleased with what he had captured of the Bukowski world.

"I just hope that, with *Factotum*, I'm a part of presenting a view of a life which I find very generous and very human. It's the strong smell of a human being, even if it has nothing to do with everyday life. People are living it. It is something real."

Frozen Food Section (2005)

Student films can be a tough road to navigate. The best of plans they've mapped out can easily veer off course when they overrun their unplanned budgets, stumble over limited schedules and locations, and often a lack of experience at all levels of a production. But when they overcome the obstacles and turn in a fairly respectable effort, well kudos and a capital A for effort.

Such was the case with the 2005 short film *Frozen Food Section*, a six minute short based on the Bukowski poem "Frozen Food Section" which appeared in the 1984 collection *War All the Time*. Directed by Andrew Menan and starring a list of raw rookies including Ben Ziegler (as Henry Chinaski, in his very first film role), Glenna Hill, Jason Woolfolk, Colin A. Borden and a whole lot of enthusiastic extras in the roles of nameless shoppers, security people, cops and faces in the crowd, *Frozen Food Section* is a crisp telling of Bukowski and his protégé Chinaski at his most sexist. With a voiceover of the poem drifting in and out and a Beethoven dirge playing an absurdist emotional backdrop, the film centers on Chinaski wandering the aisles of a supermarket contemplating the wonder of women bending over in the frozen food section. When he discovers a woman in that very position, he puts his hand where it does not belong and is immediately set upon by store employees and the police who handcuff him and give him a perp walk through a crowd of bystanders before he is tossed into the back of a squad car where Chinaski bemoans the fact that he will catch holy hell from his better half because he forgot to pick up the paprika.

Shot in Santa Fe, New Mexico at a grocery store called *The Market Place*, *Frozen Food Section* is a short, competently made bit of business that is amusing as only a Bukowski story can be, with more than a pinch of dark irony. Good, creepy fun. It's out there. Catch it if you've got six minutes to kill.

And keep your hands to yourself.

A Man/Um Homem (2005)

If you can get beyond the fact that near the end of the 26 minute Portuguese short *A Man/Um Homem*, a totally un-Bukowski like moment breaks out: an impromptu, surreal song and dance number, then what you will be left with is a competently made, gritty and claustrophobic film. It's a take on one of Bukowski's very early blatant exercises in grim dominance and submission (early being a relative word when dealing with the author's massive output), complete with an ironic twist ending that allows Bukowski to pontificate on turnabout being fair play.

As the story played out in an early '70's *Notes of a Dirty Old Man* column in the *Los Angeles Free Press*, and as part of the collection *South of No North*, *A Man/Um Homem* is the story of George, a dishwasher very much cut out of the Bukowski mold, who is interrupted at work by a former girlfriend who announces that she has just left her no-good husband. She then begins, not too subtly to seduce George, who responds with a tirade of verbal and physical abuse. That includes whipping her with a belt, slapping her across the face and burning her arm with a lighted cigarette. The girlfriend decides she has had enough of the abuse, leaves George in a semi-conscious stupor and returns to a bar where she finds her husband. She has made the decision that she was better off with her husband than with George, and they live happily ever after.

A Man/Um Homem director Laurent Simões is fairly capable of handling the gritty and misogynist elements of the compact storyline as he puts the cast: Victoria Verissimo, Ricardo Cruz, Cassamiro Alfonso and Jose Carlos, through their paces.

The Portuguese language film, complete with English subtitles, had a series of very obscure screenings in the United States and Canada as well as in Portugal, where the film captured several awards before sinking into the sunset. *A Man/Um Homem* is competent on all counts. And you've got to love the dance number.

143

The Suicide (2006)*

Director/actor Jeff Markey has this philosophy when it comes to being inspired. And in an interview he was willing to explain it in no uncertain terms. "If you're going to steal, steal from the best. That's how *The Suicide* came about. I read Charles Bukowski's short story with the same title and thought it would make a great short film."

The short film, true to Markey's admission, definitely had the Bukowski vibe and no small amounts of darkness and humor. Bukowski and death were not strangers. He wrote about the concepts of death and suicide a lot. The story *"The Suicide,"* which appeared in the collection *The People Look at Flowers at Last*, seems to get the lion's share of the credit for inspiring Markey's take, which he not only directed but starred in. But Bukowski's tales "The Suicide Kid" and "The Last Days of the Suicide Kid"—which look death and suicide square in the face—were also inspirational.

In Markey's hands, *The Suicide* takes the concept of Bukowski's world in a new, yet familiar, direction. The 14 minute short, reportedly shot off and on over a year's period at a budget of $10,000, begins with a despondent character pulling his car to a stop on a bridge and then stepping to the edge, where his contemplation of a death dive is interrupted by the arrival of two of Los Angeles's finest who, only half heartedly, talk him down and then send him on his way to a hole in the wall coffee shop. There he contemplates the futility of it all, while chugging cheap wine from a gallon jug. His sorrows are interrupted by the arrival of two masked robbers who proceed to threaten the lives of everybody in the place. But our suicidal anti hero is not having any of it, even with a gun pointed at his head. In a moment that, most likely, would have had Bukowski rolling on the floor in disbelief, our very Chinaski type disarms one of the robbers with a kick to the balls. The robbers panic and head for the hills, just as the two cops who we met at the beginning

145

burst into the restaurant and stand, exasperated, as those in the coffee shop insist that our suicidal crime fighter is a real hero. End of story.

If one were inclined to split hairs, *The Suicide* is more of a "based on the works of Charles Bukowski" rather than a literal interpretation, but the end result is so tight, compelling, dark and real that it reeks of the master's literary sense, and so is justified to carry a proud asterisk in this list of films, denoting that only some Bukowski source material was used.

Shot in and around Los Angeles, *The Suicide* blurs the line between fiction and reality. The robbery sequence was shot at local eatery *C.J.'s Café*, which, two weeks after the conclusion of filming, was actually robbed by masked gunmen in events spot-on to the film version. An even more deadly example of life mixing with art took place during the robbery sequence at the café, when a real squad car with real police pulled up just as the actors playing the robbers were about to enter the café with guns drawn. The officers, not seeing any film crew people around, assumed that were witnessing a real crime going down and jumped out of their car with guns drawn, yelling for the actors to drop their weapons. The actors did what they were told. Director Markey came running out of the cafe screaming "Don't shoot! Don't shoot! It's a movie! Don't shoot!" Cooler heads prevailed, but the real cops were quick to admonish the film crew, saying they were within moments of opening fire on the actors.

The Suicide seemed destined to join the legions of short films that disappear into the dark hole of disinterest. But Markey, recalling the aftermath of filming had other ideas. Rather than simply post the film's trailer on *MySpace* and hope for the best, Markey took the unusual step of putting the entire film on the website. Over the course of three months the filmmakers' gambit resulted in more than 33,000 hits, and a flood of favorable press.

"It's gratifying to have people see the film and respond to it they way they did," recalled the director. "I think putting up the entire film was more interesting. The response we received with *The Suicide* proves that there is an audience out there for these kinds of stories. So although not many doors in Hollywood were opened, many hearts around the world have been."

146

Pink and Tender (2008)

The short film *Pink and Tender*, based on the Bukowski short story "Rape! Rape!" which appeared in the collection *Erections, Ejaculations, Exhibitions and General Tales of Ordinary Madness*, may be extremely hard to find. So difficult, in fact, that the best the film's director Erik Boccio could offer was a link to a low quality copy of the original YouTube posting from a number of years back, and an explanation of its scarcity on any platform.

"This film has been unlisted for 10 years," he explained. "I don't have access to my original drives at the moment, so hopefully this will do."

The mystery deepens, but here's what we know. The storyline, typical in-your-face Bukowski, finds the protagonist walking down the street when he spots a sexually charged woman who immediately drives him into a madness to assault her. He follows her to her apartment, tracks her to her floor and then goes from apartment to apartment, finding unappetizing tenants along the way, before coming upon the room where the woman is seemingly awaiting him and tempting him. He grabs her, rips off her clothes and violently rapes her before stepping away to shower off. The woman gives every indication of liking to be raped. He steps out of the shower only to be met by two police officers who the woman, still breathless from the violation, tells the officers she was raped by him. Now in a psychological stupor, the man is led away in cuffs and jailed. Shortly thereafter, his victim drops all charges and the man is freed to wander the street in a what-the-fuck daze before being drawn back to the woman's apartment and up to her floor. But this is where Bukowski makes a hard psychotic left turn. Our anti-hero, instead, go to the apartment of a less attractive woman who opens the door, invites him in and another assault ensues as we fade to black.

Pink and Tender ("Rape! Rape!") was Boccio's very first film, and he was very much in synch with the Bukowski psyche, he recalled. "*Tales of Ordinary Madness* was the first Bukowski book I ever read. I was 19 years old, growing up in New York. Bukowski was the scoundrel that every young man wanted to be, at least artistic young men who were lost emotionally and morally. I went on to read several of Bukowski's other books, but one story from *Tales* always stood out for me. That was 'Rape! Rape!'."

From the film's inception, it was evident that Boccio's independent nature would be a driving force, especially when it came to the obvious challenges of making art out of violent rape. "In the mainstream sense, this would have been a very difficult story to tell. As a 25 year-old man with no desire to profit off the film or to appease the masses, I made the film I wanted to make."

The film Boccio wanted to make, while intended to be a literal translation of Bukowski's story, was not a carbon copy. Missing from the film is any reference to the lead character's medical test, which precedes the main body of the story. Also, some character juggling eliminated the apartment tenant with the special needs child who has a pivotal element in Bukowski's story, but in the film that family is totally erased in favor of a generic woman who gets in on the action. Moreover, there are the fire-breathing antics of the rape victim which are nowhere to be found in the original story. Boccio related that those bits of artistic license were part and parcel of his approach to the film.

"Pink And Tender was, for the most part, a literal translation. I altered some details that I felt would read better on screen. I knew I wanted to make an experimental film, so I removed all the dialogue to allow the images and the music to speak for itself. I also changed the title to something more personal to avoid the complications of promoting a film called *Rape! Rape!*."

Boccio went about casting *Pink and Tender*. The director acknowledged that there were lots of actors looking for work at that time, but conceded that casting the film, which would star Martin Friedrichs and Shanti Carson, would be a challenge. "Initially I was concerned that casting was going to be difficult, especially as a 'no budget for the love of film' project. I put out a call on the Craigslist talent section and I remember being shocked at the amount of interest, even when being upfront about the controversial subject matter."

Total shooting time for *Pink and Tender* was a microscopic day and a half—one day devoted to shooting city and apartment sequences, and another half day for courthouse exteriors and for what Boccio cryptically called "the fire-play inserts."

The director chuckled at the question of budget. "Other than lunch for the crew there was no budget, none. I used my own apartment, whatever camera equipment we had and borrowed some police uniforms from a friend's feature [that was] shooting at the same time."

Pink and Tender had a short coming out, playing one lone festival, The Long Island Film Festival, in 2007. Boccio recalled that the response was mixed at best. "Experimental is a tough category to get a rise out of an audience. The screening was all about sharing with the cast and crew. I never made the film for the general public. It was made, quite simply, to get my hands dirty as a director, and to pay homage to a brilliant writer."

Boccio was quick to elaborate on *Pink and Tender's* decade plus absence from the internet, emphasizing that it was not so much a matter of the subject matter as it was the technology. "We shot the film on a Panasonic Mini DV Camcorder. Based on how far digital filmmaking has come, the film just feels amateur and dated."

But in the end, Boccio felt that *Pink and Tender* was an important step in his career. "This was my first film. I'm glad I didn't pull any punches with this one. I know there would be much resistance to telling this story in 2022."

Syn Szatana/Son of Satan (2008)

The power of Bukowski's work to travel so compellingly on an international stage is typified by this truly amateur, yet quite good, made-in-Poland short film *Syn Szatana*, based on the Bukowski short story "Son of Satan." Though not the first attempt to adapt this particular story of childhood violence and how the concept of anger is passed down the generations, *Syn Szatana* is a worthwhile seven minutes of your time.

Directed by Sandra Tomalka and with a miniscule cast, the film is faithful and earnest: a literal black and white take on the Bukowski story, no more no less, but one that shows a lot of promise. For what would turn out to be the director's very first film, Tomalka would be humble and to the point about her maiden film voyage, as quoted in *Delford Cinema.org.*

"The film was shot in Katowice, Poland in 2002. At the time, none of the crew were professional actors or filmmakers. We were amateurs, just passionate young people who wanted to tell this disturbing and moving story by an extraordinary writer, Charles Bukowski."

Owing to the challenges facing a short film by total unknowns, *Syn Szatana* would languish in obscurity before receiving a nominal release on the festival circuit in 2008 and would be receive several regional awards in Poland.

Nedgang Och Fall (2009)

In the name of honesty being the best policy, here is the brutally honest assessment of the Swedish short film *Nedgang Och Fall* (*Decline and Fall*) by the film's director Hampus Bystrom. "It's not very good. But we were young and over our heads. It was an interesting film to make. You can watch the film. Here it is."

So I did.

Bookended by grainy, surreal war footage, Bystrom's 15 minute interpretation of Bukowski's story "Decline And Fall," originally published in the *Los Angeles Weekly News* in 1973 and later as part of the collection *Hot Water Music* in 1983, it tells the story of a bar patron entertaining the bartender with a story that he insists is true. Then we are immediately in the backstory as it is being told. It is a straightforward look at a very Chinaski-like man who pays a visit to his equally lay about friend and his wife. After pontificating about what they consider to be the fatalist approach to life, the film turns voyeuristic as the friend has sex with his wife while our hero watches. They return to their visit as if nothing out of the ordinary has happened, and are served a hearty meal by the wife. When the visitor compliments the wife on the meal, they reveal that what they are eating is human flesh, and, to prove the point, they take him to the kitchen and open a freezer to show him the remains of a recent murder victim they have been consuming at their leisure. The man freaks out, vomits and attempts to leave, when he is blindsided by the wife and ends up having sex with her as the husband watches. Back in the present, the bartender flips out at the tale which the customer now insists was made up. But the bartender continues to freak out, takes a gun out from behind the counter and shoots the customer, ending the tale with the question of how reality and fantasy can play out in Bukowski's world.

The visceral and over-the-top nature of Bukowski's tale was the ideal vision for the ever -candid Bystrom who, at age 19, had made a handful of Super 8 films, and by his own admission "had a teenager's attitude toward sex and violence and being provocative."

"Bukowski had been on my radar for a while," he reflected. "My father had some of his books, and spoke about him with admiration. So I read his copy of *Post Office* and I liked it. I picked up a copy of *Hot Water Music* and started to read it. Bukowski's stories in this collection were over the top and grizzly, which appealed to my teenage lack of subtlety."

Bystrom recalled having found a particular psychological kinship with the story "Decline And Fall." "The fact that it was so vile and over the top appealed to me. My approach was fairly literal, but I wanted to use the aesthetics I was infatuated with at the time: long, slow takes. I thought the combination of a somber and serious style with the exploitive material would clash in interesting ways."

The shooting schedule for *Nedgang Och Fall* was three days, with a budget he would dance around by saying, "We paid the actors and the technical support and equipment." It would finally end up being five days, due to circumstances Bystrom candidly and uneasily explained to the author.

"The story contains a sex scene, and we (the filmmakers) were very wary of it. But I figured that to us, as young and cocky guys, that element of the film would be no problem. Most of the shooting seemed to go pretty okay, but we completely lost control over the sexual aspects on the set. The only excuse was that we were 18-19 year old kids who didn't know what we were doing, and we lost control and left this inexperienced young actress in the deep. She was the only woman on the set, and the male actors were making sexual remarks and jokes and we didn't have the authority to shut them down. We thought the scene had gone okay, but after the shooting day was over the actress sent us a text message saying she didn't want to continue filming. She wasn't molested or anything, but the scene was fairly intimate, and she just wasn't prepared for it. I think she felt she couldn't trust anyone on the set, and that the director was clueless. Since we had devoted an entire day to filming her scenes, we felt the entire film was lost. Luckily we found another actress to step in on short notice and we reshot all the scenes with her."

Bystrom conceded that he learned a hard lesson in navigating the world of Bukowski. "Lesson learned. Sexual content is hard to handle, and trust between actor and director is vital in such matters. We weren't responsible to the actress, and we should have had more control over the set."

Nedgang Ach Fall had a token festival appearance at the Radar Hamburg Film Festival where, owing to the inconsistent sound system on the print and at the festival itself, was a critical failure. That added to the emotional scars Bystrom continued to feel after this attempt at Bukowski cinema. "I've always loved movies, but the experience left me somewhat scared. Instead of learning from it, I felt a complete lack of confidence, and felt I just didn't have what it takes to make movies."

After what he considered the 2010 failure, Bystrom retreated into obscurity for the next 12 years, surfacing occasionally to contribute visual political campaigns to Swedish candidates, but always in the back of his mind was the haunting experience of *Nedgang Och Fall*. "Since that time, nothing I have done has been as serious as what we attempted with *Decline and Fall*," he said.

For what would turn out to be Bystrom's only known film credit to date, the director seems to have an idea of who should do what and when. The cast: Liam Landberg, Isak Landqvist, Anders T. Peedu, Jamie Jill Sevelflod and Utas, do a fair to middling job of portraying the characters, and the filmed-in-Stockholm locations make gritty use of the black and white film.

Critically, *Nedgang Och Fall* is acceptable fare, despite Bystrom's downplaying of the effort. It is rough in spots with the look and feel of a first film, with the art-house war footage that were not in Bukowski's tale, but overall, despite Bystrom's pessimism, it is an okay adaptation of Bukowski's story.

Bystrom, who is currently attempting a film comeback on a project that remains well under the radar, still looks back on his first film adventure as an abject failure both as a film and as a representation of Bukowski's story. "I've learned that being provocative should not be one's main goal in adapting a story. It led to a film without any real personality. The world of Bukowski's character has very little to do with my own experience, and even if I feel that a filmmaker and a writer can and should try to expand their imagination and look at strange things, there has to be some point of contact between deeper emotions and the story. I just didn't find any emotional contact, and as a result the film ended up being purely an adolescent, stylistic experiment. I don't think it did the proper justice to Bukowski."

A .45 to Pay the Rent (2010)

Reality check: most, but in all fairness not all, teenagers really don't have a clue. Mykee Morettini was an exception to the rule. At 17, growing up in Illinois, Morettini was a film junkie with several short films of his own already in the can. And like most teenagers, he was up for just about any reasonable or unreasonable challenge.

That's when the Bukowski short story "A .45 to Pay the Rent" entered his life. Morettini was the first to admit that when it came to Bukowski, he did not get it. "I was not aware of Bukowski at all," he told the author. "It was part of a collection of short stories that my friend was reading for his high school literature class, and he convinced me to make a movie so he wouldn't have to write an essay about the book."

"A .45 to Pay the Rent" appeared in the 1972 collection *Erections, Ejaculations, Exhibitions and General Tales of Ordinary Madness*. It is, on the surface, a prototypical Bukowski look at the dead-end lives of dead-end people, in this case a dysfunctional family headed by a lowlife who has decided that selling drugs rather than working for the man is the appropriate job option. He rants endlessly about his life and society's woes to a submissive wife and a bright child who seems impervious to the chaos around her. It is the father/daughter interchange throughout the story that is, by Bukowski standards, heart warming, and proves a subtle anchor to the dark reality of the characters' lives.

All this piqued Morettini's interest toward taking the tale to the screen. "I liked that it was a gritty and hard edged story, and that it dealt with difficult subject matter. I thought that making the movie would be interesting to tackle, as a 17 year old kid."

Morettini proudly acknowledged that, at 17, he was doing Bukowski on the cheap, with more than a nod and a wink to both John Waters and Roger Corman. His a take on *A .45 to Pay the Rent* was done with a screenplay by a school chum and an extensive use of Bukowski's

157

own words as dialogue from the original story. "It was a no-budget production. I was the only crew. I was the director, filming on a cheap mini DV camcorder, and editing. We had no lighting, no audio gear, no crew, no budget. The approach was this weird, lowfi, homemade look."

Shot in and around North Chicago, with an all male cast, even for the two female roles, that included Jay Sawyer (who also wrote the screenplay), Max Cvijovic and Kyle Verbeke, it was cut-to-the-basics filmmaking, but with more than a touch of adolescent enthusiasm and daring which covered for any lack of filmmaking skills.

The filmmaker looked back on the filmmaking process of with fond memories.

"A good deal of the film takes place inside a home, shot around North Chicago. We had no female actors, so all the female roles were played by teenage boys. And it wasn't a matter of winking to the audience. We played everything very straight. We shot a scene at a grocery store without permission. We just walked in and started filming until the store people saw what we were doing and shut us down. We shot a scene where our drug dealer makes a sharp turn onto the highway and another car almost drives into him, and we did that scene for real on the highway. I hopped out of the car while two friends drove both cars around the bend. We did a lot of stuff like that. For most of the scenes in the car featuring dialogue, the shots were either dubbed due to the noisy audio, or while the car was stationary. I had to pitch up the one actor's voice because he was playing a small child, despite being 15 years old. Making this movie was all kinds of odd, but it was fun to just shrug and say 'given the limited resources we have, how can we make this happen?'"

Morettini acknowledged that they were playing a bit fast and loose with Bukowski's original story, and that its length, clocking in at 29 minutes, was a bit long by short film standards. "There's a lot we don't see in the film. A good deal of the film is a heated exchange between the drug dealer and his wife, which was in keeping with the original story. At 29 minutes it's a long film, but that was by design. We wanted to let things simmer and linger."

In teenage hands, *A .45 to Pay the Rent* is an interesting exercise, full of the energy and youthful enthusiasm one would expect from young kids attempting Bukowski. The film never had a public airing, but is available on *Youtube.com's Mordacious Films* for interested viewers. Years after the fact, Morettini hopes for a lot of looks. "Hopefully, people discover it and get a kick out of how weird and fringe it is."

Dr. Nazi (2011)

The opening sequence of the French short film *Dr. Nazi* is an explicit montage of a woman showing it all and intimating the rest, over a narration—in English—describing the meaning of the word "fuck." If that is not a blatant introduction to a Bukowski film, I don't know what is. But in the hands of French film director Joan Chemla, this is where things took an unexpected turn.

"Dr. Nazi," written by Bukowski in 1972 and making appearances in the *Los Angeles Free Press* and *Nola Express* before becoming a part of the collection *South of No North* in 1973, despite a bit of ogling at its onset is a fairly sedate tale—by Bukowski standards. It offers up the conceit of Chinaski, the ultimate negativist, with some physical ailments. He decides to see a doctor—a confessed former Nazi—who seems just as interested in airing his psychological quirks and dark backstory to Chinaski than in tending to his patient's physical ailments. They engage in an ongoing dual therapy that carries on over a series of visits by Chinaski, as he continues to see the doctor for a seemingly never-ending series of ailments.

Directed by Chemla, the cast includes Nicholas Clerc, Celine Samie and Bernard Waver. This 15-minute short is a deft mixture of subtle and obvious that highlights elements of the Bukowski/Chinaski character and the characters' psychological framework. The considerable technical sleight-of-hand is surprising, given the fact that *Dr. Nazi* was only Chemla's second film after an early career in law and journalism.

Mermaid of Venice (2011)

If you are even a marginal viewer of Bukowski cinema, then Gregory Flitsanov's 23-minute short film *Mermaid of Venice*, based on that ever-enticing Bukowski short story "The Copulating Mermaid of Venice Beach" may smack of old news, and you would be right. Several filmmakers have attempted to make cinematic sense of unflinching tale of drunks and dead bodies, some with seemingly more enthusiasm than others. Flitsanov, in a quote from his entry in *Bukowski Forum.com*, had been less than thrilled at the prospect.

"I usually don't like doing adaptations. But I was just too inspired by this particular story. I just had to do it."

Mermaid of Venice, shot at various Los Angeles locations including Venice Beach, and with a cast that toplined Tom Demar, Guy Mack and Irena Eremina, is essentially a take on a simple, albeit bizarre storyline. Similar to other takes on the story, it is about two down and out drunks steal a corpse out of a mortuary transport van, discover it is the body of a woman, have sex with the corpse and then dispose of the body in the ocean. It is a crisp, fairly well acted outing, focusing just as much on the lifestyle of the two losers as it does with the horrendous deed. It is a well done, small effort that is readily available on several internet platforms. This take on the all too familiar Bukowski story is not necessarily a must-see, but if you happen upon it in your travels, you could do a lot worse.

Mask (2011), Live True Dewars AD (2013) and Levi's Jeans Ad(2013)

If Bukowski had been around to witness the one minute short unveiled in Japan just in time for the Christmas shopping season, he would have probably toasted the occasion with a tall, cold one and then proceeded to laugh his ass off. Because *Mask* was everything he seemingly spent his entire life railing against. It was his work morphing into a blatant commercial for a woman's cosmetic line, filmed by a Chinese born high style, glitzy director Kari Wai Wong and featuring actress/model Sandrine Pinna. In the space of a minute it had, at least on a subliminal level, turned Bukowski into a corporate pitchman.

By 2011, this is what it had gotten to. In the time-honored tradition of pop culture icons becoming the darlings of Madison Avenue's corporate exploitation, even such an unlikely personage as Charles Bukowski was not immune to being associated with a commercial brand or, as in this case, three.

First up. *Mask.*

Mask was "inspired"—according to the press releases trumpeting the *Shu Uemura* beauty products line—by the poetry and the vibe of the 1974 collection *Burning in Water, Drowning in Flame*, a collection that mirrored Bukowski's drinking, womanizing and just plain living his life in early 60's Los Angeles.

Despite the director's word to the contrary, while *Burning in Water, Drowning in Flame* is the title of the collection, no singular poem seems to exist with that title.

Or does it? Abel Debritto, who has written more about Bukowski and his work than just about any author or researcher, was more than willing to share his two cents on the elusive *Mask* ad.

"This is a bit tricky. The poem "Burning in Water, Drowning in Flame" was first published in a little magazine called *Second Coming* in

163

1972. It was in the collection entitled *Burning in Water, Drowning in Flame,* and finally it was in the collection I put out in 2017 called *Storm for the Living and the Dead.* I doubt very much that the director had seen the original magazine publication. Since the commercial came out before my book, my guess is he probably referred to the overall vibe of the book *Burning in Water, Drowning in Flame* that came out in 1972."

Mask, the commercial, has been locked away from prying eyes since its 2011 release, and is considered "private property." One site that teased at having it available, subsequently backed off and said that it was not available. A few frames did appear, though, showing the actress savoring the result of makeup application in deep hues of red and blue, images that seem to emphasize the fantasy and a subtle sensuality that highlights the product, but in a tasteful, non-Bukowski way. In an interview that appeared in the website *Shu Uemura*, Wong Kari Wa, the director, painted a circumspect and glossy picture of the Bukowski connection. "I wanted to get across a message celebrating life and carrying a positive energy. I thought that the contrast between red and blue in the makeup pigment reflecting the hot and cold was ideal."

Reality check readers: If Bukowski was reading this… You fill in the blank.

In the meantime, corporate America was not through with Bukowski. In an either totally appropriate or totally inappropriate move, depending on where your ethics lie, *Dewars*, the liquor conglomerate, decided to release a commercial extolling the virtue of their latest concoction *White Label Scotch Whiskey* to the accompaniment of an emotional reading of Bukowski's poem "So You Want to Be a Writer," a late in life Bukowski poem from a 2003 collection entitled *Sifting Through the Madness for the Word, the Line, the Way.* At a running time of 1:49, it is a montage of middle-American, urban corporate hustlers working their way through the challenges of manhood and making it. It is quite good in its execution, and the rendition of Bukowski's poem is effectively told in an encouraging, though world-weary manner. It is a solid, albeit morally questionable, exercise for a couple of reasons.

Nowhere in this paean to alcohol consumption is Bukowski given credit as the author of the poem. And irony of ironies, Bukowski was a confirmed beer drinker who, according to all reports, never drank scotch. Unlike *Mask*, you can easily find the commercial *Live True* in a lot of places on the internet. So take a look and form your own opinion.

And while you're at it, contemplate this: Bukowski's poem "The Laughing Heart," is playing in the background while a bunch of internationally-inspired, well scrubbed youth go out to change the world—in a series of quick cuts that clock in at a cool 1:00. That's all in the name of selling Levi's blue jeans to illustrate their slogan, *Go Forth*. Again no credit is given to Bukowski for having done all the grunt work of creating the poem, which was originally another late in life work written in 1993. It was published as part of a collection entitled *The Laughing Heart* in 1996, and again in 2002 in a collection entitled *Betting On The Muse*. It is a poem in which Bukowski reflected on his life as only he could.

His estate probably didn't even get a pair of blue jeans for signing on the bottom line. Can you see Bukowski walking through his life in a pair of Levi's? I know, neither can I.

Breakfast with Bukowski (2011)

Bukowski's work has been ripe for interpretation, and nowhere is this more evident than in the balls out, quite funny, animated short *Breakfast with Bukowski*, a four minute bit of business from filmmaker Greg Runnels that follows Henry Chinaski in the midst of writers' block as he struggles to find a title for his latest work. In very short order, Henry goes to the track looking for inspiration, wins a couple of races, has an unsuccessful encounter with a woman, buys a six pack, is chased down the street by a vicious dog and finally, downing a very warm beer, stumbles upon the elusive title: *Love Is a Dog from Hell*.

That Runnels chose animation as his cinema weapon of choice would try the director's patience as he recalled in a *Sonoma International Film Festival* interview. "I was working on it for seven years. Animation is very expensive. Trying to get the idea of animation with the right animator also took a while. I went through a series of animators trying to get what I wanted. Then I ran into an animator named Frank Cromer who is a real Bukowski fan who brought a lot of nuances I never would have thought about. The first time I approached him on this he told me it was his 'God and Jesus' moment."

Runnells acknowledged at the festival interview that "I was a Bukowski fan for a long time, and I always saw Bukowski as an adult animated character. For me, he was the perfect animated character."

The Laughing Heart (2012)

Tom Waits languidly reads the Bukowski poem "The Laughing Heart" in that world weary, trademark voice of his, while the lines of the poem and simple sketch/line drawings play out, floating over the reading in kinetic, animated fits and starts—two minutes and out. It's as simple as Bukowski-inspired cinema gets. Like Bukowski, it's quick, to the point, and, emotionally, surprisingly effective at making its point.

Directed by Travis Carr, it is a convincing rendition of "The Laughing Heart," a poem reportedly written in the last months of his life in 1993 and published in 1996 after his death in a collection entitled *The Laughing Heart,* and also as part of the collection *Betting on the Muse* in 2002. This short film is proof that Bukowski, all bluster and image aside, could be deep.

Charles Bukowski's Nirvana (2013)

I'm not the one to go to if you're looking for a pull quote, empty praise or equally empty hyperbole. I call them as I see them, and if there's collateral damage or bruised egos, so be it. Having said that, I can honestly report that a 4:53 minute short film, *Charles Bukowski's Nirvana,* born of a Kickstarter campaign that netted a $4,000 budget, is easily the most memorable, surreal, melancholy and, yes, loving tribute to Bukowski and his work I have seen to date.

"Nirvana," as originally written by Bukowski, made its earliest known appearance in the collection *In The Shadow of the Rose* in 1991. It was followed a year later in the collection *The Last Night of the Earth Poems*, a year after that in the collection *Run with the Hunted*, and, in 2016, in the collection entitled *Essential Bukowski Poetry*. "Nirvana" was Bukowski at his last stages of life: a time for contemplation and in which his long time alter ego Henry Chinaski was the universal everyman. In a way it was in keeping with the outsider persona of the writer, and more importantly, in was a lyrical commentary on where he was at and where he was going.

The story of "Nirvana" is the tale of Henry riding on a bus through a snowy wilderness, jotting down his thoughts and dreams in a notebook. The bus makes a stop at an in-the-middle-of-nowhere rest stop where Henry observes and contemplates a waitress and others, perceiving their attitudes, hopes and dreams. A moment caught in lyrical time flashes before him as he gets back on the bus that travels down a snowy road.

There's a lot of emotion and contemplation for the reader, as there must have been for the short film's director Patrick Biesemans. There is a true sense of mature cinematography at work in *Nirvana* as actor Greg Starr, without saying a word, is the perfect quiet Don Quixote as Henry. His silent subtle physical presence goes through the motions as "Nirvana," read by singer-songwriter Tom Waits, plays in the background. Biesemans' film is all sentiment and beautiful emotion. It is that good.

Not surprisingly, the director unearthed a deeply emotional and personal tale behind the making of *Charles Bukowski's Nirvana*. "I was alone on a road trip in California and I had the Tom Waits album *Orphans* playing. At one point in the trip the cut of Waits reading the poem "Nirvana" came on. It instantly resonated with me. The sense of being untethered but also being okay with it."

At that point, Biesemans had only had limited exposure to Bukowski, and would not read much of Bukowski's work until after making the film. In hindsight, he reflected on the fact that not being what would be a big Bukowski fan most likely worked to the advantage of the film he would make. "Most of Bukowski's community of readers envision a more down and out world than what was portrayed in my film. And I can understand why. It's an intoxicating world to live in, but it wasn't right for *Nirvana*. Not all of Bukowski's work is about hard days and boozy nights. With "Nirvana" he painted a simple picture of holding onto the moment for as long as you can because who knows what comes next. The challenge was painting the right picture, as opposed to what you would expect to see in a Bukowski film."

Charles Bukowski's Nirvana had, by short film standards, a fairly leisurely three months of prep and three months of post with three days of actual filming in the middle. Biesemans readily acknowledged that "it was a production that was done on very little money and lots of favors. You come to expect a certain look from a Bukowski film. What I wanted to do was paint an almost Norman Rockwell portrait of being aimless. It had to have the look of a certain quality."

Biesemans acknowledged his hopes and dreams for the film in a conversation with *Moving Poems.com*.

"We loved the opportunity to pay tribute to Bukowski, and by association, Waits, by creating a short film, inspired and complimentary to a great poem. It is a focus on atmospheric qualities that Waits presents with his voice and Bukowski with his words. It's a story revolving around the quiet moments that inspire great writing. It's a surreal yet welcoming artistic representation of the world. It's a love letter to travelers, writers, singers, storytellers and poets."

In conversation, the director would admit that making *Charles Bukowski's Nirvana* also struck a personal chord. "It certainly taught me to enjoy the moment, not only in film production but in my own life."

Fuck the Forest or I Don't Want to Die Here
Eaten By Animals (2013)

First of all, I can vouch for the fact that Bukowski never wrote anything with the title "Fuck the Forest or I Don't Want to Die Here Eaten By Animals." I've got the internet research and the inherent eyestrain to back me up. But if you want to know the origin of the film that spawned this 18-minute French romp which is trumpeted as "based on the works of Charles Bukowski,' simply go to your well-worn copy of *Women* and turn to chapter 30. There, in all its glory, is Bukowski's comedic romp as city slicker Henry Chinaski, lost in the woods and dealing with two women who know exactly what they want.

The result, for director Lewis Aithbert Ashton was a loose and, by degrees, fairly amusing interpretation of the *Women* chapter which holds together pretty well. It's true to the character, true to the vibe of the original story, and, for an extra, added attraction, contains two vintage Jefferson Airplane tunes in the soundtrack. When directing, Ashton, doing double duty as Henry, is quite good at portraying everybody's favorite rebel poet as a babe lost in the woods.

The Big Pot Game (2013)

Remember those stodgy educational films you had to sit through? They usually sprang those on you in the fifth or sixth grade under the assumption that puberty was on the horizon, and they wanted to head off any potential problems at the pass. Remember how those films, usually narrated in a too serious voice by a male professor done up in coat and tie, were punctuated with line charts and stick figures? Remember how you ultimately did not learn much that you didn't already know, but that, in hindsight, they were always good for a laugh and they got you out of the last hour of class?

What if the narrator of those films had been Charles Bukowski? And what if he had a very anti-establishment agenda? Enter *The Big Pot Game*, a 10-minute short that is alternately campy, dated and featuring a curmudgeonly Henry Chinaski going on at length about a pet peeve: The devil weed.

Director Tim Thelen, an apparent New Age/Meher Baba advocate whose skimpy filmography (three total short films) all land squarely in the realm of conservative/enlightened thinking and feature Tom Saunders as a pontificating explorer of vices in the world, is, in fact, a literal translation of the Bukowski short story of the same name written in 1967 for the underground newspaper *Open City* in his *Notes of a Dirty Old Man* column and subsequently included in the collections *Erections, Ejaculations, Exhibitions and General Tales of Ordinary Madness* (1972) and *Tales of Ordinary Madness* (1983).

The crux of the film is Henry weaving in and out of a laughable hip Hollywood party and an even more laughable encounter with two terrible, stoned hippie impersonators, before the film lapses into some hippie love stock footage and some race track footage while we learn more than we wanted to know about Bukowski's feelings on the chemical and alcoholic vices of society. *The Big Pot Game* is readily available on

175

several apps. That there were no festival appearances or awards is not surprising.

The Big Pot Game was obviously meant to further a message and an agenda. What it does do is offer up a perfect lead in to a screening of *Reefer Madness*.

Run to the Sea (2014)*

In the cause of making this book as complete as possible, I offer up *Run to the Sea* with a great big asterisk. Pure and simple, this is a 10-minute surfing film, nothing more, nothing less. What qualifies this as a Bukowski film is actually a bit of a gimmicky cheat. At the beginning of the film we get Tom Waits reading a portion of Bukowski's "The Laughing Heart," a mere fragment clocking in at under a minute. End of Bukowski tie in. What we are left with is a lot of surfing footage backed by, admittedly, two very good Nina Simone tunes. Why director Dylan Stott even bothered with the Bukowski bit remains a mystery.

Bukowski (2014)

Bukowski, the 2014 biopic of Charles Bukowski by actor/director/ producer/choose your hyphenate James Franco, is like an episode of the series *Law and Order.* Before we cue the guitar riffs/bluesy trademark intro, here are the facts of the case.

Franco always seemed to have a film option in the fire, and it isn't surprising that he would eventually cast his sights upon the notion of a biography film of Bukowski's early childhood, high school years, struggles with an abusive father, disfiguring acne, alcoholism and his first tentative steps at becoming a writer. On paper, the cast, headed by Josh Peck as Bukowski, Tim Blake Nelson as Bukowski's father and Shannen Doherty as Bukowski's mother, appeared more than up to the task.

In a 2013 interview with *The Credits.com* Franco gushed about the prospects for the film, and his admiration for Bukowski. "I've always been a fan of Bukowski," he declared. "I think artist coming-of-age stories always resonate with me. This movie is not an adaptation of *Ham on Rye.* It focuses on his childhood.

Speaking for his filmmaking brother, Dave Franco was thrilled at the prospect of a Bukowski film, as he explained in a quote that appeared on *Fatnancysnewsdiet.com.* "One of my favorite books of all time is *Ham on Rye* by Charles Bukowski. Hopefully this will amount to something. It's pretty dark, and it's not going to be a movie that appeals to wide audiences. But we love it so much."

Easy as pie?

Not necessarily.

Well into the 2000's, Bukowski's work, especially his earliest books, had long since been optioned to just about anybody, famous or obscure, who could cut a deal with the writer, often at a cut rate price. Notable film director Paul Verhoeven had snapped up the rights to *Women.* At the other end of the spectrum was a little known British art dealer-entrepreneur-hustler (chose your hyphenate) named Cyril Humphris. Long time Bukowski confidant Neeli Cherkovski vaguely remembered in an interview that "He (Bukowski) sold off the rights to Ham On Rye to some British guy," but that was all.

According to a number of accounts, Franco's attempt to turn Bukowski's early life into *Bukowski* the film became serious in 2009 when he entered into a deal with Humphris to acquire the film rights to *Ham on Rye*. That deal that was set to expire, according to Humphris, in 2010. It was at the stroke of 2010 that things began to unravel.

In 2009, right about the time Humphris and Franco were finalizing their deal, *The New York Times* reported that Humphris was finishing up his own script for *Ham on Rye*, and was in the process of casting and signing a production deal with Amblin Entertainment. Subsequent research indicated, however, that not only had a *Ham on Rye* script not been registered, or for that matter seen, but there was nothing to indicate that Amblin Entertainment was going to produce the film.

But as Franco continued to prep his film, inconsistencies, or as it is sometimes called, "typical Hollywood business," began to surface. If this were truly a *Law and Order* episode, what happened next would have been cause for a mistrial.

The first bombshell came courtesy of Neeli Cherkovski in a conversation when he matter of factly said that Franco did, in fact, have designs on making a film of *Ham on Rye*. "Franco wanted to make a movie out of *Ham on Rye*. Franco came to me and offered me a tiny bit of money to pretend that they were using my book (*Hank: The Life of Charles Bukowski* which was published by Random House in 1991) when, in fact they were using *Ham on Rye*. It was just bullshit and it made me sick."

Cherkovski's allegations of something funny going on would be given credence by Franco himself in a blog for *The Huffington Post*, cited in *Bukowskiforum.com*, where he was quoted as saying he was "using an undisclosed biography as source material."

Cherkovski's allegations of dirty dealings would be backed by a conversation with Abel Debritto, the noted author/editor/historian of several non-fiction Bukowski books and a confidant of Bukowski's widow, Linda. "Franco's film is based on a script by one Adam Rager. At one point, Linda asked me to read the script that Franco's agent had sent her. I compared the script to the book *Ham on Rye* and it was an obvious rip off, including some passages that were reproduced almost verbatim. Some scenes were identical to *Ham on Rye*. I told Linda as much, and shortly after that Franco was sued. I don't know what happened after that. Linda never told me."

As the questions and controversies began to swirl around the project, Franco, in 2013, actually began filming on January 22 in Los Angeles. The production would shoot for two weeks, take a break and resume filming in March. By the time Franco's *Bukowski* was essentially completed it became evident that all was not right between Franco and Humphris. According to *The Hollywood Reporter*, Humphris emailed Franco regarding the legality of his production, seeing as how the film rights deal between Franco and he had expired in November 2010. Franco responded with "I'm doing a little project with my NYU colleagues based on one of Bukowski's biographies." Perhaps sensing there were dark legal clouds on the horizon, Franco, according to *The Hollywood Reporter* story, did several press interviews in which he insisted that his film was not based on the Bukowski book *Ham on Rye*.

In April 2014, around the time the film had been completed and Franco was looking for distribution, Humphris filed a lawsuit in federal court alleging that Franco had adapted the book *Ham on Rye* without having the film rights to the book. In his lawsuit, Humphris was seeking an injunction against the film's release and compensatory damages. Throughout the course of the trial, interesting arguments were presented, such as that facts can't be copyrighted but facts done in a creative manner can. What is or is not "fair use," long a staple designation in the publishing world, was very much discussed. Franco's legal team suggested at one point in the proceedings that an investigation be made into the book *Ham on Rye* to determine the factual basis for the novel.

As the trial proceeded, *Bukowski* remained in limbo, with only "announced" and "TBA" status attached to any mention of the film. The inevitable backlash about the quality of the film was beginning to surface. The trial was not doing Franco or his take on Bukowski any good in the public mind. Finally, in April 2014, a settlement was reached, and both sides submitted paperwork to have the lawsuit dismissed with prejudice. *The Hollywood Reporter* stated that there was a settlement, but the terms of that settlement would remain confidential.

It would be a hollow victory for Franco and *Bukowski*. A 2014 release date was soon announced—that was very light on specifics. Two years later, in 2016, a second release date was floated. As late as 2020 yet another tepid release date for the film was announced. Word along the gossip line was that *Bukowski* had been shelved and was currently in Hollywood limbo. There have been no recent reports of a release for the film. It appeared that the lawsuit had done its work.

Bukowski researcher Abel Debritto could only speculate as to whether this Bukowski movie would ever see the light of day. "I was under the impression that it was actually never released. Nobody I know has seen it."

And so in a creative sense, a cinematic sense, who knows?

Love Is a Dog from Hell (2014)

Johannes Hochgatterer had no illusions about making a very short student film based on the Bukowski poem "Love Is a Dog from Hell." As he explained, it was ingenuity triumphing over just about everything else.

"The budget was $200, and that went entirely toward the payment for the location. It was just two actresses and I, and we shot their scenes in a few hours. I borrowed the cameras from a friend."

This four-minute short, directed by Hochgatterer and starring Chante Holloway, Amanda Vannucchi and Ryan Timberlake, is easily on the top of the list of the most unseen Bukowski films. Doing this book is the only reason I got access to *Love Is a Dog from Hell*, and Hochgatterer offers that all the secrecy is for a good reason. "I only show the film to people privately. I can't (legally) make any money off it because I'm using a poem, footage from other films and music that I don't own the rights to."

The long and short of *Love Is a Dog from Hell* is this: There are two women in an apartment—one moving out, one moving in. Their memories play out amid mental and emotional moments in staccato segments of other films, as the off-screen narrator reads the poem "Love Is a Dog from Hell." By Bukowski standards the poem plays as personal, jagged and introspective. It starts abruptly ends with a violent denouement.

Hochgatterer became aware of Bukowski and his world at age 17 when he saw the films *Factotum* and *Barfly*. Bukowski's books sealed the deal for him and his admiration grew for what he considered the authors' "anti hero image, quiet stories and sense of humor." When it came time for Hochgatterer to stretch his wings while a student at the New York Film Academy, he did not have to look any further than the Bukowski collection *Love Is a Dog from Hell* to find inspiration. "*Love Is a Dog from Hell* was the very first book by Bukowski that I read. I loved the title, so in that sense it was a no brainer. Bukowski being my favorite author, it made sense choosing one of his poems as a short. The reason I chose to adapt the poem that also happened to be the title of the book was because it didn't feel like it should be adapted in the literal sense. It didn't feel like I had to force myself to put Bukowski's words into images. It felt like a chance to adapt something that invited me to do something on my own."

Hochgatterer's seemingly contrary and progressive approach was to "create this rough hand held type of footage with raw, unclean dialogue, the thoughts and feelings that are not necessarily expressed in the poem." The director's non-literal look at Bukowski was expressed in off-kilter cutaways of the films *The Obscure Object of Desire* and *Electra Glide in Blue*, driven by the pulsating rhythms of The Beatles song "Drive My Car." Hochgatterer staunchly defends this admittedly surrealist approach to *Love Is a Dog from Hell*.

"I was not interested in making a literal translation of the poem into film," he explained. "To me, the poem was rather complex because it was so unapologetically personal. There is not a single line in it that is aimed at the reader."

The conceit of Bukowski and his work was totally lost on actress and Second City Chicago alum Vannucchi. "I am ashamed to admit that I had not heard of Bukowski until Johannes approached me with the project. I didn't read or hear the poem until I watched the finished film."

Once filming began, she was up to speed on how the director wanted things done. "The unique thing about this film was that there was no written dialogue. Johannes gave us a few actions and the circumstances of the scene, and then Chante and I completely improvised the dialogue. We filmed the live action sequence in a matter of hours. It was Johannes, Chante and I—with the camera. The improv just flowed."

Hochgatterer concedes that *Love Is a Dog from Hell* could have been better. As a student film early in his career, it is easy to find faults and things he would like to have done differently or better. But at the end of the day, he is satisfied with the results of a film that most people will never see.

"When you're adapting something by Bukowski, all you end up with is realizing, over and over again, how great a writer he was and is. The best you can do is to make your own thing and honor the man the only way that's appropriate, and the only way that he would honor his heroes. Which is to not give a shit."

Hit Man (2014)

It seems a given that a modicum of passion and admiration for Bukowski and his work would be a prerequisite for attempting to make a film of one of his works. But when tracking down *Hit Man* director Nicholas Kohut, the overall impression was rather ho-hum.

"I was a big fan of Bukowski in college, but not so much anymore," he said. "He's a great poet, but the content doesn't resonate with me anymore."

"Hit Man" the short story, which appeared in the *South of No North* collection, is a pretty straightforward and compact bit of business. There's a meeting in a bar between a sullen hit man and a smarmy husband who is in the process of hiring him to kill his wife. They haggle a bit, trade a bon mot or two, money changes hands and the hit man goes off to off the wife—which he does, as we fade to black.

When a friend of Kohut brought the story to his attention, the better to fulfill an undergraduate school requirement, the budding filmmaker sensed that it would be easy pickings, creatively. "It was a literal translation. We pretty much adapted the exact story. We changed a couple of minor details in the dialogue, but it is what Bukowski wrote."

That approach would be maintained throughout the four day shoot, budgeted in the $6,000-$8,000 range because of film cost and processing. Kohut put his cast: Robin Brecker, Dan Fivestone, Dave Polgar, Heather Cole and Samantha Heaps, through a fairly regimented filming process. "We were shooting on film and had hardly any money, so we couldn't waste too much time getting things perfect," the director remembered. "A one-minute-long take was a lot of money we couldn't get back, so we had to limit our takes, and sometimes the performances just weren't there. Overall, the film was a big learning experience."

But it was an experience, flaws and all, that Kohut came away from with positive memories. "This was the film I learned to build a proper crew on. We had 15 amazing crew members come together to make this film, and I was able to sit in the director's chair to guide the magic as it unfolded because of everyone's collaboration."

Hit Man would ultimately get limited exposure. "We did a few small screenings in Philadelphia. But the film took a long time to finish and we ended up not liking it too much, so we didn't push it. That's always an issue when you take too long to finish a project. We grow as artists, and some projects become irrelevant quicker than others."

Hit Man is out there. Track it down and see for yourself.

The Strangest Thing Just Happened (2015)
and Sitting on a Fire Escape Eating Eggs (2015)

Yes it does happen this way: One good idea gets out into the world and two different filmmakers from different parts of the film spectrum think it's so good that, unbeknownst to the other, both take the same idea and run with it. Especially when the idea is a Bukowski tale.

The Strangest Thing Just Happened is aptly named. For openers, it is neither based on a Bukowski short story or poem. It is, in fact, based on a story that the author told during the taping of the 1987 documentary *The Bukowski Tapes*. In that segment, Bukowski recounts the day he was sitting at the window of his apartment, dealing with the absolute worst hangover on the planet when, suddenly, a body falls from above, past his window and splatters onto the street.

That's the story. See a movie in that? Dennis Dicker, aided and abetted by producer-musician Dennis Coggins did, and the result is a nifty bit of no budget business shot entirely in front of a green screen featuring various psychedelic images and music. Dylan Barnes, as Bukowski, contemplates what has just happened, as a dark monologue of the adventure plays out. It's reportedly surreal, disorienting stuff.

Another version, and one upon initial viewing a frantic, darkly comedic take on the exact same story is the five minute, $500 wonder *Sitting on a Fire Escape Eating Eggs*. Directed by Michael Stevantoni and starring Jonathan Peacy and Erin Kay Smith, this film doesn't waste any time. Bukowski is shown cooking eggs in the aftermath of a terrible hangover and is sitting on the fire escape when all of a sudden a body falls from above. Bukowski freaks and runs into his apartment to frantically report the incident to his unbelieving better half, Linda. After a futile attempt to convince her, our hero grabs Linda and they go to the fire escape. She looks down, sees the splattered remains on the ground, freaks, runs back into the apartment and vomits into the toilet. This definitely falls into the category of guilty pleasure. You'll feel guilty for laughing, but it will easily tickle your sadistic funny bone.

Director Stevantoni acknowledged in *Bukowski Forum.com* that he was taking certain liberties with his film. "It was the casualness that drew me to the story. While I did want to go a little bigger with it, it's not authentic Buk. I think it should viewed more as 'the world of Bukowski,' but with a different character."

Bukowski reportedly swore this was a true incident in his life. And in the hands of two filmmakers from different sides of the world, it was definitely stranger than fiction.

Vessel (2015)

Vessel is a smart, enticing little film that takes up the challenge of a Bukowski poem that is off the beaten path. The poem, "On Seeing an Old Civil War Painting with My Love," which appears in the collection *The Roominghouse Madrigals*, is pure thinking man's Bukowski: all imagined observation mixed in with the struggles and madness of a woman during war time. The poem skips back and forth in a manner that would seem to challenge any filmmaker to make sense of it.

Filmmaker Mimi Cave took up the challenge, and the result is *Vessel*, a 13-minute dark journey of a dysfunctional relationship between a mother and child, woven into whole cloth from an excerpt of the poem. It follows them through the day and night horrors of life. The film is often surreal in execution and context, and features snippets of the Bukowski poem over ballet-like underwater sequences. Starring Denna Thomsen and Aidan McGraw, it is a smart interpretation of a Bukowski poem that is not typical Bukowski.

Warm Face/Cold Place (2015)

Caridad Cole sees Bukowski differently than most of us do. She's a fan and she is familiar with his work and image. But she is also politically and socially astute, so when she looks at Bukowski she also sees an astute observer of the world. "I am a huge Bukowski fan," Cole acknowledged in an email exchange. "He is my favorite American poet."

And while a film school student at Bard, the occasion of creating a student film brought her to Bukowski in a big way in the guise of the Bukowski poem "The House," which first saw light in the collection *Burning in Water, Drowning in Flame*. "Warm Face/Cold Place is a literal translation of the Bukowski poem "The House" and how I chose to interpret it," she explained. "I chose 'The House' because Bukowski was a master at shining a light on issues most people would have rather not seen. 'The House' exemplified that. Bukowski often criticized the socioeconomic hypocrisy in America. The country was experiencing extreme political unrest during the time I made this film, and I was feeling much of the same things Bukowski wrote about. I had a clear image in mind when reading this poem and so I had to bring it to life."

Warm Face/Cold Place, clocking in at a shade under six minutes and starring Peter Anchel and Caroline Petty, juxtaposes Bukowski's harsh look at society as he watches a house being built with two young kids who attempt to build a home with their own hands using the debris they find around them. Ultimately, they find solace in each other, even as their attempts to build a shelter fall down around them. Effectively dystopian in design, and ripe with the reality and attitude of the times, the film, complete with a robot to text voiceover of Bukowski's poem, is a minor cinema statement, effectively made.

With a budget of $350, and the one location being a New York City brickyard, Cole knew she would be challenged. "The only challenge I had was that I committed to using only our physical surroundings, no outsourced props or help. It was just me and my two actors. They had to really attempt to build a structure around themselves, using the debris. No matter how many times things fell apart."

Bluebird(2016)

When British director Oliver Ridge was working his way through academia in England, he would literally hold his nose at the prospect of reading traditional poetry. "It was all about the angst of seducing maidens in the 1700's," he recalled in an interview with *EricRobertsIsTheMan.com*. "I couldn't stand it, or pretty much poetry in general at that point."

But Ridge did an abrupt 180 when a friend turned him on to the poetry of Charles Bukowski. "Bukowski was the ugly side of poetry. I was totally into it. And I have to admit it, when I read the poem "Bluebird" I cried. I knew it would make a great film someday."

Someday arrived some years later when Ridge relocated from London to Los Angeles where he began to embark on a film career, first as a producer on the critically acclaimed film *Last Days of Summer*. But Ridge would find himself with the itch to be more creative, and that's when "Bluebird" was once again on his emotional radar. In a *Hollywood Revealed* interview he explained the beginnings of the project. "I was impatient to be in creative control. I think that desire brought 'Bluebird' back to me. The emotions are universal." He further explored his attraction in an interview with *Cliché Magazine*. "They [the characters] transcend gender, wealth and race. There is a loneliness in being a human being and that we are all in it together, regardless of what's on the outside."

Ridge nailed it. "Bluebird," which appeared in the 1992 collection *The Last Night of the Earth Poems*, easily highlighted Bukowski's vulnerability as somebody who was quite familiar with living in pain and using the familiar coping mechanisms of alcohol, women and cigarettes to attempt and deflect the hurt inside.

Bluebird would be Ridge's directorial debut which brought him some nervous anticipation, but when he managed to get Oscar-nominated actor Eric Roberts to do his film, Ridge admitted, in separate interviews with *Eric RobertsIsTheMan.com* and *Cliché Magazine,* that the pressure was really on. "It was all about timing. Eric is considered ungettable because he's always working. But I managed to get to him and get him. I won't lie. There was some nerves. I remember the night before we started shooting *Bluebird*, it dawned on me that the next day I would be directing an Oscar nominated actor. But at the end of the day, it wasn't intimidating because I knew the material inside and out."

Ridge's approach to making film sense of *Bluebird* was also a bit progressive. Nearly all of the ten minute running time of the film, written by Ridge and Don Mercer and with a three person cast of Eric Roberts, Sonalli Castillo and David Cady, effectively jumps back and forth between Roberts, as a down on his luck Bukowski/Chinaski character known only as The Man, and two lovers dealing with their own pain and anguish in another level of society. The silence is finally broken at the fade, when Roberts' character in voiceover/close up recites "Bluebird" into the camera.

Cinematographer Colton Davie, in a quote from his own website, *ColtonDavie.com*, recalled the shoot as surprisingly stress free. "For a first film, it was a pleasure to shoot. The film contained no dialogue and, as such, relies heavily on visuals to compare and contrast the two stories of longing, one down in the belly of Hollywood and the other high in the hills. We worked with a small crew and limited lighting to create striking images on a tight schedule and a tight budget."

Ridge, in *EricRobertsIsTheMan.com*, acknowledged that his small film was rewarded with a powerful Eric Roberts performance. "It was an honor to work with Eric. Eric had no ego. He was down to play. Eric was down to be in that ugliness."

At the end of the day, *Bluebird* emerges as a legitimate diamond in the rough: a powerful homage to Bukowski at his most sensitive and reflecting. It is a first rate work that is out there on an app or two, but has mostly slipped below the radar. Ridge, in a story in *Film14.com*, was quick to downplay any notoriety connected to him because it is Bukowski- inspired.

"The film is a labor of love and is not for profit in any way, shape or form. I love Bukowski and I wanted to make the film to get more people to read his work."

Girl on the Escalator (2016)

One has to give Brazilian filmmaker Kayhan Lannes Ozman credit. In a space of just under five minutes, with his adaptation of the Bukowski poem "Girl on the Escalator," he has come up with the perfect distillation of Bukowski in all his image, attitude and underhanded comedic humor.

The set up is simple, and immediately strikes at elements of both eroticism and comedy. In the poem that has appeared in the collections *The Night Torn Mad with Footsteps* and *The Pleasures of the Damned*, Bukowski gets on an escalator in back of a young couple. She is "hot," and with the aid of strategically-placed scenes of the woman as perceived by the poem, she comes across as a vapid shell-a broad characterization aided by no small amount of misogyny. The cast, which includes Nicole Della Costa, Breno Moreira and James Scott as the voice of Bukowski, play things fairly straight and broad, which mixes well with Bukowski's laconic tones and the amusing clichés that the poem, in voiceover, trots out.

The subject matter and the interpretation of Bukowski's attitude toward women has made *Girl on the Escalator* a bit of controversial item, to be sure. But it appears that the filmmaker's intentions were straightforward and consistent with the Bukowski ethos.

Whether or not one agrees with the political incorrectness of it all, *Girl on the Escalator* is well worth the five minutes you will have invested in viewing it. It is a well-made exercise that will most certainly have people agreeing to disagree.

Alone with Everybody (2016)
and Alone with Everybody (2017)

Perhaps the most fatalistic and ultimately depressing thing Charles Bukowski may well have ever written is the poem "Alone with Everybody." The poem appeared in the *Love Is a Dog from Hell* collection, and in it Bukowski squeezes every conceivable drop of desperation, hopeless and loneliness onto the page.

Not surprisingly, the dour nature of the poem has made it a prime choice for the cinema world. For filmmaker and musician André Viuvens, interpreting Bukowski's poem was a one man band effort in which he is credited as director, voiceover actor and an assortment of technical titles. The resultant two minute montage of mostly black and white archival footage over his reading of the poem is quite effective in conveying the sense of isolation and hopelessness that Bukowski's poem projects. As an emotional, albeit bleak, interpretation, it works.

As it turned out, *Alone with Everybody* would once again surface the following year with a take by director Adrián Suárez. His version, equally stylized and sensually focused, has a heightened sense of emotion and reality that plays in the face of the dour nature, including glimpses of humanity and hope that, in keeping with the tone of Bukowski's poem, add real creative heft to this slightly more than two minute exploration.

Suarez, in conversation with *Directors Notes.com*, expressed a deep affinity for Bukowski, and, in particular, the poem "Alone With Everybody." "Among all the poems of Bukowski, I chose "Alone with Everybody" because it seems to me that it reflects a part of society. His poems are very direct with a fresh language, free of any artifice. That made me feel inclined toward this poem and author."

Given that admiration, Suarez acknowledged that he had his work cut out for him. "The challenge was to achieve a compact, highly visual piece of work without production resources. Once I developed the idea,

I spent eight months finding everything (equipment, locations) I needed. Everything about this film was informed by the theme of the poem which makes much reference to the sensual, to the flesh. I had to respect the poem. *Alone with Everybody* is a personal project where I had the freedom to make what I really wanted."

Piss (2018)

The poem "Piss" only mentions the act in the title and in the first few lines of the poem before veering off into a tale of sewing and making clothes. Make sense so far? Well here's where things get interesting.

Then student filmmaker Nelli Toth decided to take the title and the more outrageous possibilities of anything connected to the Bukowski image and create a whole new storyline that, according to the five minute short film's credits is "based on the poem Piss." It's all a bit of a shakedown, if you ask me, but the result is a fairly humorous take on Bukowski's lifestyle and bodily functions.

Piss is a true missing link, so much so that when the author managed to track down Ms. Toth, who is currently working her way through film school, she was surprised that anyone had even heard of her 2018 student film. "There are people out there who are watching student films? Oh my God! I can't even convince my friends and family to watch them!"

In Toth's hands, *Piss* is fairly straightforward. Bukowski is sitting at his typewriter, in his shorts, doing what Bukowski always does, which is stare at the typewriter and wait for inspiration to strike. When all of a sudden, his drunk girlfriend staggers into the apartment and reports that she could not hold her water and just pissed in the elevator. Bukowski being Bukowski, he immediately wanders out into the hallway and opens the elevator to find his girlfriend's puddle, just as two other apartment dwellers walk into the elevator, see Bukowski in his shorts and spot the puddle. A sheepish Bukowski walks out of the elevator, back to his apartment, sits down at his typewriter and begins to write.

The minimal cast of John Mertens and Katrina Phillips plays it all very big and broad but, surprisingly, also straight in execution.

"I was always a big Bukowski fan," Toth remembered. "When I was growing up in Hungary I used to listen to recordings of his poems before bed. The thing I loved most about him was his raw honesty and that he was able to find beauty in everyday ugliness, in things we often judge or ignore."

Toth's Bukowski "jones" continued into 2018 when, now in the US and attending film school, the poem "Piss" became her muse. "I had the book *Betting the Muse* sitting next to my bed for many years, with the poem "Piss" marked with yellow sticky tape. So making a short film of that poem came to mind because it was relatively simple and low budget."

And in the case of *Piss*, Toth saw the opportunity to take the conceit of the poem and turn it into a story—albeit a good one, into something that was totally unrelated to the narrative of the poem. She turned sheepish when asked to explain why she did it that way. "I didn't realize that was what I was doing. It was not my intention. I thought by putting the title of the poem and Bukowski's name in it, it would explain whose story will be on screen. I read that poem and just imagined the story I came up with visually. I tried to stay true to the poem. It was not my intention to come up with a whole new story."

Toth recruited her cast through an ad in Backstage Magazine. Katrina Phillips, a professional dancer by trade, signed on for the role of Mary, the drunken girlfriend. In the pivotal role of Charles Bukowski, John Mertens said yes, but he would admit in an email interview later that he was reluctant at first. "I had been a fan of Bukowski's novels for a long time. I don't admire him as a person but I admire him as a writer. I don't think writers come any more honest than CB. I had stopped doing student films several years before. But I made an exception because of the role and the subject."

For her part, Toth would continue playing fast and loose with her "different take" on the film, making Charles Bukowski and his persona the central character in the film. "I wanted viewers to know that the film was based on the poem by Charles Bukowski so I put his name at the beginning of the film, and then at the end in the credits."

Given its student-film origin, it is not surprising that *Piss* was very much a guerrilla production. Shot in 10 hours, largely in a one room studio apartment, with a skeletal cast and crew of fellow film students who were there to dodge the real life requirements of the other apartment dwellers and go the extra mile to make sure the film was as close to the period of the story as possible. Among other things, that meant tracking down a very old typewriter for the sequences in which Bukowski is hunched over, writing.

Toth remembered one particular challenge to her drive for authenticity: "I remember one of the biggest issues was finding out what kind of cigarette Bukowski smoked in those days. But I couldn't get it in time, so we ended up using the gaffers' red Marlboro."

During the filming, Mertens discovered that playing the real life Bukowski was more of a challenge than playing his alter ego Henry Chinaski would have been. "I knew I couldn't be Bukowski. I played the scenes and the character knowing it was Bukowski, but I didn't try to play Bukowski. I don't know if that makes sense, but that's how I thought about it. I felt like I knew the life the character lived and the way he viewed the world, and I tried to live it before the camera."

Piss, which had a couple of very limited film school-related screenings but can be found on *filmfreeway.com* and *Vimeo*, had Toth looking back on *Piss* both critically and with no small degree of reverence. "The short feels like a long-paced student film with a very small amount of set ups. But I still feel the essence and humor of Bukowski can be found in there. Bukowski's style has definitely left a mark on me. Do I think the film captured the essence and spirit of Bukowski? I hope it did."

No Leaders Please (2021)

Joan Gratz is nothing if not a purist when it comes to her art. Armed with a special technique best described as "clay painting," a technique of animating clay-based oils and painting an image as the camera rolls, she has brought a sense of eloquence to a series of short, award winning films.

When it came to approaching the world of Bukowski with a two minute animated short *No Leaders Please* based on the poem of the same name which originally appeared in the collection *The Pleasures of the Damned*, the artist knew exactly what she was in for, as she explained in an interview with *The Peninsula.com*. "Its form was explicit, as I tried to interpret the message from his poem through the work of other artists [Jean-Michel Basquiat, Banksy and Keith Haring]."

In an email exchange with Gratz, the filmmaker explained that her approach to making *No Leaders Please* was a slow, deliberate and painstaking process in which she applied lots of clay, blended colors and etched in fine lines, and shot a frame at a time. "The technique involved painting an image directly in front of the camera, making a change to the image and then shooting another frame."

"No Leaders Please," is read in voiceover by Tom O'Bedlam, and plays effectively with the perceptions we have about Bukowski. The film is a soothing interlude during which other true creatives and their work play out in snapshot-like moments over the introspective reading of the poem. At two minutes, *No Leaders Please* makes a direct point and the impact of Bukowski's work is clear. At two minutes it was just right and just enough.

Gratz described that her approach to *No Leaders Please* was to take a different path from the preconceived notion of Bukowski. "I was inspired by the poem. Though he has been referred to as the 'poet laureate of the low life,' this poem is about invention and reinvention. Unlike

Marc Shapiro

some of his work, which is often dark and cynical, this is a poem that celebrates creativity."

Death Is Smoking My Cigars (2021)

This is a smart, crisp and just plain well done bit of animated business, wrapped up in a package just a shade under three minutes.

The premise of *Death Is Smoking My Cigars* is based on the poem of the same name that appeared in the Bukowski collection *The Last Night of the Earth Poems*. It is an odyssey, a coming to Jesus biographical moment in which Bukowski deals with reality of being a struggling writer and bucking the odds while being stalked by the specter of death. Death, personified, smokes the writer's cigars while taunting him with the notion that he will most certainly fail, and that he will ultimately come to him.

In the hands of director A.J. Leon, *Death Is Smoking My Cigars* is a deep dive into all the emotions and attitudes that have always circled Bukowski's world; the themes of death, immortality, writing, literature and low life urban culture are dealt a breakneck but spot on pace. The animations, a mixture of hand drawn and digital elements shot through with dark shading, are coarse, yet ideal. *Death Is Smoking My Cigars* is a deft piece of Bukowski filmmaking, and we're led down the path of his life accompanied by Tchaikovsky's Symphony No. 6.

The Icecream People (2021)

Scenario: Charles Bukowski and twin German women. If that isn't the set up for a bit of debauchery and lowlife antics, I don't know what is. There is a Bukowski story or poem in there somewhere. In the form of the short film *The Icecream People*, that tale was being made.

Helmed by the German born twin sisters Antonia and Francesca Pollak, making a Bukowski film seemed inevitable. "We've always been very fond of Bukowski," the sisters said in an email conversation. "Mostly because of his striking description of Los Angeles, and the fact that, like us, Bukowski is German born."

Actor Justin Sintic, who plays a decidedly "different" vision of Bukowski, said that, as a long time Bukowski reader, he found a lot to admire in his words. "I've always marveled at his ability to turn the messier part of the human experience into poetry. I'm reminded of his words, 'how beautiful the interpretation of the human condition can be.'"

Given that, it is not surprising that Sintic found that *The Icecream People* struck a personal note with him. "When I read *The Icecream People*, I felt it was a poem that could be a conduit for joy. Exploring Bukowski's interpretation of youth allowed me to get closer to my own. This project came at a wonderful time as I was feeling a bit stuck creatively."

The poem "The Icecream People," which appeared in the collection *Love Is a Dog from Hell*, is that super rare feel good story in the Bukowski compendium. Bukowski, in the throws of ridding himself of the demon alcohol, latches on to the notion of ice cream and the people and society that favor the flavors, and he recognizes that they are his substance salvation. He is literally giddy at the prospect of devouring exotic combinations that, as the poem proceeds, are the cure for an alcohol-induced slowing of his libido. Ice cream represents ultimate happiness and satisfaction.

"What attracted us to the poem was the shared love of ice cream," reflected the Pollak sisters. "It's not just the eating of the ice cream but all the components leading up to it. The drive, the standing in line, the infinite and absurd flavors to chose from. The experience never lacks in fullness and that was what Bukowski echoed so beautifully in his poem."

To say that *The Icecream People* was low budget is a gross understatement. Shot over several days in and around Los Angeles with only a cell phone, a primitive microphone, a rough outline and a shot list, the Pollak sisters crafted a total anti-Bukowski image. In it Bukowski, played by actor Sintic, who totally fits the vibe, is child thrust into a wonderland, enjoying life, dancing up a storm and slurping up the ice cream while his poem plays out in lighthearted balance to this true fantasy.

Sintic acknowledged that the spartan nature of the production actually played into his portrayal of Bukowski. "It was shot over a couple of days with no fancy camera or shot list, so it kind of forced me to just go and get out of my head and into my body. I wanted to walk that fine line of pain being synonymous with pleasure. I always felt that Bukowski lived in some pain. So what does that brief moment of pleasure look like to him? How does he grapple with it? What does it look like when joy becomes the choice?"

In a way, *The Icecream People* is definitely a creative turn away from the expectedness of Bukowski's image, here transformed into pure escapism, providing a glimpse of a Bukowski that is totally removed from what we've come to expect.

Yes, this film is funny in a bizarre way, but to the Pollak sisters, it was no less a serious exercise. "More than anything, *The Icecream People* is a visual exploration of what the poem means to us. Ice cream is a metaphor for rebirth, and propels us into a whole new world. As Bukowski writes 'It's a dance between the real and the imagined, between pleasure and pain, between life and death.'"

The twin directors, who acknowledged that there was "a lot of play and freedom in the creative process," have kept *The Icecream People* in the shadows. The film has not made any festival appearances or appeared on any noticeable platforms, and that is by design. "We felt this short film just needed to exist, to be given freely to the people around us. Ultimately, it's quite liberating to see what you can create without anything at all."

Metamorphosis (2021)

One would be hard pressed to find a work by Bukowski that deftly defines his attitude and place in the universe more than the poem "Metamorphosis." It is Bukowski putting his questionable lifestyle on a pedestal and defending it to the death, although it flies in the face of the mores of polite society. Essentially, it is Bukowski living in filth and dealing with the attempts of personal and professional people to help him clean up his life. A girlfriend scrubs and fixes his bed, cuts his hair and clips his toenails. The gasman, plumber and phone man fixes what's broken and turns his life into one providing a high degree of comfort. Bukowski being Bukowski, he longs for the days when he was living in filth, as he watches his suddenly clean life spiritually and emotionally collapse around him. Soon he begins the slow process of returning to his old ways.

Metamorphosis has had a long literary life, making its first appearance in *Sparrow Magazine* in 1978 and in the subsequent collections *Play the Piano Drunk Like a Percussion Instrument Until the Fingers Begin to Bleed* (1979), *Run with the Hunted (*1993), *The Pleasures of the Damned* (2008) and *Essential Bukowski* (2016). It was almost inevitable that the poem's sense of self deprecation, feisty defiance of societal norms and the deft sense of Bukowski and his world would make *Metamorphosis* a natural for film.

And herein lies the mystery. This is what we know. The director's name is Alan Cossettini, The cast includes Andrea Beruatto, Thomas Scapinello and Diego Trillini. The film was made in Italy. In an obscure Instagram entry, director claimed he was in the editing stage of *Metamorphosis*. The film's IMDB page stated that, as of this year, Metamorphosis is still filming. Attempts to contact Cossettini and the film's production company Pale Rock Entertainment had gone for naught until literally right up to the 11th hour, when filmmaker Cossettini jumped up out of the ether of a casting director day job, and offered the whole damned story.

"I discovered Bukowski in high school," said Cossettini. "One day a friend recommended *Women*, and I was hooked. I was captured by the alliteration of drama and irony, and his ruthless and his brutally honest way of writing. After reading Bukowski all other writers suddenly seemed empty, fake and sluggish to me."

Consequently, when Cossettini decided to venture into the short filmmaking arena with *Metamorphosis*, he decided that an intricate, progressive approach was necessary. "The challenge with *Metamorphosis* was to tell the story in a single sequence shot while the protagonist moves in an out of the scene in real time, while the supporting characters move in and out in time-lapse."

Metamorphosis was shot in a studio in one day. "We sat the actor Andrea Beruatto in an armchair and built the set around him. The other actors had to enter the scene, interact with objects, do actions and then leave the scene. The supporting actors would then be sped up in time-lapse. We did a lot of rehearsals, and then just turned on the camera and everything went smooth in one single take."

So when would the world get to see the finished product? Cossettini sheepishly acknowledged that his day job has, to this point, gotten in the way. "My day job as a casting director has caused me to put *Metamorphosis* aside for a while. But I will definitely have this finished and ready to be seen by the end of 2022."

He was true to his word. As of 2023, it was released and has won awards at several film festivals.

Up from Obscurity, Down from Obscurity

The filmmakers who have attempted Bukowski all have things in common: They came from obscurity; to varying degrees, they still labor in obscurity—although some have managed to carve out quite respectable careers in front of and behind the camera. For most, putting Bukowski on film was a momentary blip on the horizon, an early attempt at expression, driven by passion, admiration, creativity and the feeling that, for whatever reason and ultimate goal, they felt it had to be done. To a person it had been a special moment—a time and place they would look back on with fondness. There were the growing pains: the mistakes they'd love to have a chance to correct, the things they got right, but their admiration for Bukowski and his work inspired them.

That I would seek these filmmakers and their memories out was universally a pleasant surprise them, and I make no bones about it: Bukowski and his work are a passion of mine.

This filmography is complete to this moment. It's a sure bet that there will be other filmmakers lurking in the wasteland who will most certainly take up the challenge of putting *Bukowski: On Film*.

Bukowski's spirit would most likely hoist a cold one to these efforts in their honor.

SOURCES

AUTHOR'S NOTES
I WROTE THIS
BOOKS
The Last Night of the Earth Poems by Charles Bukowski

FREE AT LAST
BOOKS
Open All Night by Charles Bukowski
Living on Luck: Selected Letters 1960's-1970's
Charles Bukowski: Locked in the Arms of a Crazy Life by Howard Sounes

MAGAZINES
Vice, Rolling Stone

CHEKOFSKI ON THE MYTHIC MONSTER
INTERVIEWS
Interview with Neeli Cherkovski

BUKOWSKI AT BELLEVUE
BOOKS
Erections, Ejaculations and General Tales of Ordinary Madness

WEBSITES
Dennis Schwartz Reviews.com, Film Threat.com, Medium.com

BUKOWSKI
NEWSPAPERS
Los Angeles Free Press

MAGAZINES
Malibu Magazine

WEBSITES
Bukowski Quotes.com

CLOSE BUT NO BUKOWSKI
INTERVIEWS
Howard Sounes

BOOKS
Charles Bukowski: Locked in the Arms of a Crazy Life by Howard Sounes
Visceral Bukowski: Inside the Sniper Landscape of L.A. Writers by Ben Pleasants

WEBSITES
Bukowski Forum.com, The Tracking Board.com

SUPERVAN
OBSCURE
Sussex University thesis by J.C. Farhoumand

WEBSITES
Bukowski Forum. Com Medium.com

THE GREAT FILM DIRECTOR
CRACK BUKOWSKI EXPERT
Abel Debritto

MAGAZINES
Jacaranda Review

NEWSPAPERS
Los Angeles Free Press

CHARLES BUKOWSKI: EAST HOLLYWOOD
BOOKS
Charles Bukowski: Locked in the Arms of a Crazy Life

WEBSITE
Bukowski Forum.com

HELLO I'M BACK: CHARLES BUKOWSKI IN HAMBURG
BOOKS
Shakespeare Never Did This by Charles Bukowski

THERE'S GONNA BE A GODDAMNED RIOT IN HERE
BOOKS
Living on Luck Selected Letters 1960's-1970's Vol. 2

WEBSITES
Bukowski Forum Journal

WHY BUKOWSKI GAVE HOLLYWOOD THE FINGER
INTERVIEWS
Abel Debritto, Joan Jobe Smith, Howard Sounes

BOOKS
Reach for the Sun, The Captain Is Out to Lunch and the Sailors Have Taken Over the Ship, Charles Bukowski: Locked in the Arms of a Crazy Life

MAGAZINES
Film Comment

NEWSPAPERS
New York Times

WEBSITES
Quote Park.com

MISCELLANEOUS
Bukowski: Born nto This

BUKOWSKI WRITES A SCREENPLAY
INTERVIEWS
Howard Sounes

Marc Shapiro

BOOKS
Living on Luck, Reach for the Sun

MAGAZINES
Film Comment, L'Europeo Magazine

NEWSPAPERS
New York Sun

JOAN JOBE SMITH REMEMBERS BUKOWSKI THAT WAY
INTERVIEWS
Joan Jibe Smith

THE LAST STRAW
WEBSITES
Bukowski Forum Journal

EVERY MAN FOR HIMSELF
BOOKS
Hollywood

MAGAZINES
Home Planet News

TALES OF ORDINARY MADNESS
INTERVIEWS
Howard Sounes

BOOKS
Literary L.A., Laughing with The Gods, Charles Bukowski: Locked in the Arms of a Crazy Life

MAGAZINES
L'Europeo Magazine, Twisted Image, Film Threat, Film Comment

WEBSITES
Cultural Daily.com

POETRY IN MOTION
WEBSITES
Poetry Foundation.com

THE UNTOLD STORY OF BUKOWSKI THE FILM CRITIC
INTERVIEWS
Brenda Littleton

WEBSITES
Cholla Needles Arts and Literary Library.com

THE KILLERS
WEBSITES
The Steigerwald Post.com

MISCELLANEOUS
Huntington Library Archives, Pasadena Ca.

900 POUNDS
INTERVIEWS
Fritz Fox

THE ROAD TO BARFLY
BOOKS
Looking for Gatsby,
Charles Bukowski: Locked in the Arms of a Crazy Life

MAGAZINES
Film Comment, The Word

WEBSITES
RogerEbert.com

CHARLES BUKOWSKI'S GIVE ME YOUR LOVE
INTERVIEWS
Conrad Hurtt

BARFLY
INTERVIEWS
Abel Debritto

BOOKS
Charles Bukowski: Locked in the Arms of a Crazy Life,
Reach for the Sun: Selected Letters 1978-1994

MAGAZINES
Twisted Image, Film Comment, People

NEWSPAPERS
L.A. Weekly

WEBSITES
RogerEbert.com, Bukowski Quotes.com

THE CHARLES BUKOWSKI TAPES
BOOKS
Reach for the Sun: Selected Letters 1978-1994, Charles Bukowski:
Locked in the Arms of a *Crazy Life*

MAGAZINES
Film Comment

NEWSPAPERS
The New York Times

MISCELLANEOUS
The Charles Bukowski Tapes, The Charles Bukowski Tapes Press Kit

CRAZY LOVE
MAGAZINES
Beat Scene Magazine

WEBSITES
Bukowski Forum.com, Horror News.net

LUNE FROIDE/LUNE FROIDE COLD MOON
MAGAZINES
Chroniques Des Fontaines

LOVE PIG/BRING ME YOUR LOVE
INTERVIEWS
Chris Innis

THE BEST HOTEL ON SKID ROW
NEWSPAPERS
The Village Voice

WEBSITES
Alternative Reel.com

ALL WOMEN NAMED KIKI
WEBSITES
IMDB. com, Mubi/com

GUTS
INTERVIEWS
Alex Murphy

BOOKS
South of No North

NEWSPAPERS
Los Angeles Free Press

LONELY AT THE TOP/THE BLANKET
INTERVIEWS
John Hiler

WEBSITES
IMDB.com

AMOR POR MENOS
WEBSITES
Mix Movie.com, IMDB.com

AN EVIL TOWN
INTERVIEWS
Richard Sears

NEWSPAPERS
Los Angeles Times

HORSESHOE
WEBSITES
Festival De Cannes.com, Mix Movie.com, The Guardian.com

CLIVE SAUNDERS' EXCELLENT BUKOWSKI ADVENTURE
INTERVIEWS
Clive Saunders

LOVE FOR $17.50
INTERVIEWS
Clive Saunders, Luc Niknair

GOING INTO 2000
MAGAZINES
Free Thought

THE MAN WITH THE BEAUTIFUL EYES
WEBSITES
The Marginalian.com, Psyche Films.com, MUBI.com

BRING ME YOUR LOVE
WEBSITES
Netribution.co.uk

BROKEN MIRROR MUSIC
INTERVIEWS
Andre Alfa

APPORTE MOI TON AMOUR
Bukowski Forum.com

SON OF SATAN
BOOKS
Bukowski for Beginners

MAGAZINES
Kill Pretty

MISCELLANEOUS
Chris Robinson Ottawa Animation Festival Director

BUKOWSKI: BORN INTO THIS
BOOKS
What Matters Most is How Well You Walk Through the Fire

MAGAZINES
Free Thought, Film Threat

WEBSITES
Indiwire.com

MY OLD MAN
WEBSITES
American Futures.com

FACTOTUM
MAGAZINES
Cineropa, Entertainment Weekly

WEBSITES
Today.com, Movielab.com, IGN.com, *Fox News.com*

FROZEN FOOD SECTION
NEWSPAPERS
Los Angeles Free Press

WEBSITES
IMDB.com

PINK AND TENDER
INTERVIEWS
Erik Boccio

SYN SZATANA/SON OF SATAN
WEBSITES
Delford Cinema.org

NEDGANG OCH FALL/DECLINE AND FALL
INTERVIEWS
Hampus Bystrom

A .45 TO PAY THE RENT
INTERVIEWS
Mykee Morettini

DR. NAZI
WEBSITES
Enumfrance.org, IMDB.com

MERMAID OF VENICE
WEBSITES
Bukowski Forum.com, Film Threat.com, IMDB.com

MASK AD/DEWARS AD/LEVIS AD
INTERVIEWS
Abel Debritto

WEBSITES
*Shu Umera Press Release, Shu Uemura Wong Kari Wa.com,
KCRE.com, Chicago Tribune.com, Dangerous Minds.com, Poetry
Foundation.com*

BREAKFAST WITH BUKOWSKI
WEBSITES
Sonoma International Film Festival.com, Bukowski Forum.com

THE LAUGHING HEART
WEBSITES
Filmaffinity.com, IMDB.com

CHARLES BUKOWSKI: NIRVANA
INTERVIEWS
Patrick Biesemans

WEBSITES
Moving Poems.com

FUCK THE FOREST OR I DON'T WANT TO DIE
HERE EATEN BY ANIMALS
BOOKS
Women

WEBSITES
Rate Your Music.com, IMDB.com, Bukowski Forum.com

THE BIG POT GAME
WEBSITES
IMDB.com, Bukowski Forum.com

RUN TO THE SEA
WEBSITES
IMDB.com

LOVE IS A DOG FROM HELL
INTERVIEWS
Johannes Hochgatterer, Amanda Vannucchi

HIT MAN
INTERVIEWS
Nicholas Kohut

THE STRANGEST THING JUST HAPPENED
SITTING ON A FIRE ESCAPE EATING EGGS
WEBSITES
Bukowski Forum.com, Screen Critix.com, IMDB.com, Dangerous Minds.net,

MISCELLANEOUS
The Bukowski Tapes (documentary)

VESSEL
BOOKS
The Roominghouse Madrigals

WEBSITES
Mimicave.com, IMDB.com

BLUEBIRD
MAGAZINES
Cliché Magazine

WEBSITES
EricRobertsIsTheMan.com, Hollywood Revealed.com, ColtonDavie.com, Film 14.com

GIRL ON THE ESCALATOR
BOOKS
Night Torn Dead with Footsteps, The Pleasures of the Damned

WEBSITES
Bukowski Quotes.com, Film School Rejects.com, Open Culture.com

ALONE WITH EVERYBODY
BOOKS
Love is a Dog from Hell

WEBSITES
Directors Notes.com, Bukowski Quotes.com, IMDB.com

PISS
INTERVIEWS
Nelli Toth, John Mertens

WEBSITES
Film Freeway.com

NO LEADERS PLEASE
INTERVIEWS
Joan Gratz

WEBSITES
The Peninsula .com

DEATH IS SMOKING MY CIGARS
BOOKS
The Last Night of the Earth Poems

WEBSITES
Death Is Smoking My Cigars.com, MUBI.com, A.J. Leon.co,

THE ICECREAM PEOPLE
INTERVIEWS
Antonia Pollak, Francesca Pollak, Justin Stimic

METAMOROPHIS
INTERVIEWS
Alan Cossettini

WEBSITES
Best Poems.net, Poeticus.net, IMDB.com, Bukowski.net

About the Author

New York Times bestselling author Marc Shapiro has written more than 60 nonfiction celebrity biographies, more than 24 comic books, numerous short stories and poetry, and three short-form screenplays. He is also a veteran freelance entertainment journalist.

His young adult book, *JK Rowling: The Wizard Behind Harry Potter,* was on *The New York Times* bestseller list for four straight weeks. His fact-based book *Total Titanic* was also on *The Los Angeles Times* bestseller list for four weeks. *Justin Bieber: The Fever* was on the nationwide Canadian bestseller list for several weeks.

Shapiro has written books on such personalities as Shonda Rhimes, George Harrison, Carlos Santana, Annette Funicello, Lorde, Lindsay Johan, E.L. James, Jamie Dornan, Dakota Johnson, Adele and countless others. He also co-authored the autobiography of mixed martial arts fighter Tito Ortiz, *This is Gonna Hurt: The Life of a Mixed Martial Arts Champion.*

He is currently working on the follow up to *Beatle Wives*: *The Women Who Married the Men We Fell in Love With* with *Beatle Kids* for Riverdale Avenue Books.

Other Riverdale Avenue Books Titles by Marc Shapiro

Beatle Wives: The Women the Men We Loved Fell in Love With

Word Up: The Life of Amanda Gorman

*Keanu Reeves' Excellent Adventure
An Unofficial Biography*

Hard Work: The Greta Van Fleet Story

*Lorde: Your Heroine,
How This Young Feminist Broke the Rules and Succeeded*

Legally Bieber: Justin Bieber at 18

*You're Gonna Make It After All:
The Life, Times and Influence of Mary Tyler Moore*

Hey Joe: The Unauthorized Biography of a Rock Classic

*Trump This! The Life and Times of Donald Trump,0
an Unauthorized Biography*

The Secret Life of EL James

The Real Steele: The Unauthorized Biography of Dakota Johnson

*Inside Grey's Anatomy:
The Unauthorized Biography of Jamie Dornan*

Marc Shapiro

Annette Funicello: America's Sweetheart

Game: The Resurrection of Tim Tebow

Lindsay Lohan: Fully Loaded, From Disney to Disaster

We Love Jenni: An Unauthorized Biography

Who Is Katie Holmes? An Unauthorized Biography

Norman Reedus: True Tales of The Waking Dead's Zombie Hunter,
An Unauthorized Biography

Welcome to Shondaland:
An Unauthorized Biography of Shonda Rhimes

Renaissance Man: The Lin Manuel Story

John McCain: View from the Hill